GH00383939

Brazilian
Pantanal

Alex & Gardênia Robinson

Credits

Footprint credits
Editor: Jo Williams
Maps: Kevin Feeney

Managing Director: Andy Riddle
Content Director: Patrick Dawson
Publisher: Alan Murphy
Publishing Managers: Felicity Laughton,
Jo Williams, Nicola Gibbs
Marketing and Partnerships Director:
Liz Harper
Marketing Executive: Liz Eyles
Trade Product Manager: Diane McEntee
Accounts Managers: Paul Bew, Tania Ross
Advertising: Renu Sibal, Elizabeth Taylor
Trade Product Co-ordinator: Kirsty Holmes

Photography credits
Front cover: Dreamstime
Back cover: Dreamstime

Printed in Great Britain by CPI Antony Rowe,
Chippenham, Wiltshire

Every effort has been made to ensure that
the facts in this guidebook are accurate.
However, travellers should still obtain
advice from consulates, airlines etc about
travel and visa requirements before travelling.
The authors and publishers cannot accept
responsibility for any loss, injury or
inconvenience however caused.

Publishing information
Footprint *Focus Brazilian Pantanal*
1st edition
© Footprint Handbooks Ltd
May 2012

ISBN: 978 1 908206 640
CIP DATA: A catalogue record for this book
is available from the British Library

® Footprint Handbooks and the Footprint
mark are a registered trademark of Footprint
Handbooks Ltd

Published by Footprint
6 Riverside Court
Lower Bristol Road
Bath BA2 3DZ, UK
T +44 (0)1225 469141
F +44 (0)1225 469461
footprinttravelguides.com

Distributed in the USA by Globe Pequot Press,
Guilford, Connecticut

The content of Footprint *Focus Brazilian
Pantanal* has been taken directly from
Footprint's *Brazil Handbook*, which was
researched and written by Alex and Gardênia
Robinson.

Contents

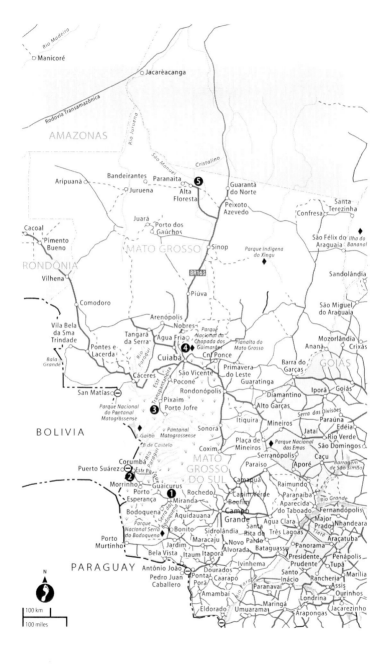

The Pantanal, which is an enormous seasonally flooded wetland on the borders of Brazil, Paraguay and Bolivia, is the best place in the Americas for spotting wild animals, and one of the best places in the world to see birds. Capybara, anaconda, peccary, giant otter, metre-long macaws and ocelots are common sights and it is even possible to see that most elusive of South American mammals, the jaguar. At the end of the dry season, between June and August, the number of water birds, raptors and parrots has to be seen to be believed. Visiting the wetlands is easy with a large choice of camping tours from Campo Grande, Cuiabá, Corumbá or Miranda; or there's the more comfortable option of staying at one of the *fazenda* ranch houses that are increasingly opening their doors to tourists. Families with children will enjoy the little resort town of Bonito, which is famous for its clear-water rivers and caves, and makes a good base for visiting the Pantanal.

The Pantanal lies within two Brazilian states: Mato Grosso do Sul and Mato Grosso. Until the second half of the 20th century these were little-explored wildernesses of table-top mountains, *cerrado*, savannah and dense rainforest. The famous British explorer, Colonel Percy Fawcett, was lost, and perhaps murdered, in the forests of the Xingu, and Theodore Roosevelt contracted a fatal disease on an expedition here in previously uncharted territory. These days, even the Pantanal is grazed by cattle, and the great Amazonian forests of northern Mato Grosso state are steadily giving way to soya beans, planted for the vegetarians of the USA and Europe and the kitchens of China. However, substantial pockets of forest still remain for now, particularly around the Rio Cristalino near the town of Alta Floresta, where one of the best jungle lodges in the Americas can be found.

Planning your trip

When to visit the Brazilian Pantanal

The Pantanal is worth visiting at any time of year. However, the dry season from June to October is the ideal time to see wildlife as animals and birds congregate at the few remaining areas of water. This is also the breeding season, when birds form vast nesting areas, with thousands crowding the trees, creating an almost deafening cacophony of sounds. The white-sand river beaches are exposed, *jacarés* bask in the sun, and capybara frolic in the grass. It is during these months you are most likely to see jaguars, however, July sees lots of Brazilian visitors and the increased activity decreases the chances of sightings. From the end of November to the end of March (wettest in February), most of the area, which is crossed by many rivers, is subject to flooding. At this time mosquitoes abound and cattle crowd onto the few islands remaining above water. In the southern part of the Pantanal, many wild animals leave the area, but in the northern Pantanal, which is slightly higher, the animals remain.

Getting to the Brazilian Pantanal

The Pantanal can be reached from both Mato Grosso and Mato Grosso do Sul states. In Mato Grosso access is from the capital city, Cuiabá, which has an airport. In Mato Grosso do Sul, access is from the state capital, Campo Grande, or from Corumbá on the border with Bolivia (both cities have airports); or from the little cattle ranching town of Miranda (connected to the rest of Brazil by bus and train), which lies between them.

There are three ways to visit the Pantanal. The cheapest (and most popular with backpackers) is to take an **organized tour**. These involve camping, perhaps with a night in a *fazenda* (ranch house), and a range of activities, including hiking, canoeing and wildlife and birdwatching. Guides tend to emphasize light adventure and have reasonable general knowledge of the Pantanal but poor knowledge of specific plants or animals.

Another option is to organize a tour through a **fazenda**. Although some are very modest, *fazendas* are generally comfortable with air-conditioned rooms and good home cooking. Many (if requested in advance) can organize decent wildlife guides who know English and scientific names for birds and animals. *Fazendas* can also be booked through tour operators, such as **Brazil Nature Tours** in Campo Grande (see page 61), **Explore Pantanal** in Miranda (see page 61) or **Pantanal Nature Tours** in Cuiabá (see page 81).

It is also possible to visit the Pantanal on a **self-drive tour**, by hiring a 4WD in Cuiabá or Campo Grande. Those considering this option should speak good Portuguese and stick to the two principal dirt roads that enter the Pantanal: the Transpantaneira in Mato Grosso and the Estrada Parque in Mato Grosso do Sul.

For further information on the Pantanal, consult www.braziltour.com, www.brazil tourism.org, www.turismo.ms.gov.br and www.sedtur.mt.gov.br.

International flights into the Pantanal Flights from the USA or Europe tend to come via Rio de Janeiro or São Paulo with airlines such as TAP, www.flytap.com. Make sure you arrive two hours before international flights. It is wise to reconfirm your flight as departure times

Don't miss ...

The numbers here relate to the map on page 4.

may have changed. ▸▸ *For airport tax, see page 19. Prices are cheapest in October, November and after Carnaval and at their highest in the European summer and the Brazilian high seasons (generally 15 December to 15 January, the Thursday before Carnaval to the Saturday after Carnaval, and 15 June to 15 August).*

Transport in the Brazilian Pantanal

Visiting the Southern Pantanal → *For details see Mato Grosso do Sul, page 45.*
Access to the southern Pantanal is from Campo Grande (see page 45), Miranda (see page 51) and Corumbá (see page 53), all in Mato Grosso do Sul.

Campo Grande offers the bulk of the rock-bottom budget tours. But these are of significantly lower quality than those you'll find on offer in towns like Miranda.

Corumbá, near the Bolivian border, was once the capital of backpacker tourism in the Pantanal but, although many budget agencies have offices here and cheap tours are readily organized, the town is now used more as a departure point for boat trips. ▸▸ *See page 61.*

Miranda lies half way between Campo Grande and Corumbá at the turn off to Bonito. It is still a Pantanal ranching town free of touts, and the best of the *fazendas* (ranch house safari hotels) are situated close by. There are two excellent operators and the town is friendly and relaxed. Although there are excellent *fazendas* off the Estrada Parque road, there are also an increasing number opening up to tourism around Miranda. These include the stylish, upmarket **Refúgio Ecológico Caiman**, the closest thing central Brazil has to a Mexican hacienda (and similarly beloved of the chic) and **Fazenda San Francisco**, which is probably the best spot in the entire Pantanal for big cats, especially ocelot, which you can almost be guaranteed to see. ▸▸ *See pages 57 and 58.*

Many of the tours and some of the *fazendas* lie off a dirt road running off the BR-262 Campo Grande to Corumbá highway. This road, which is known as the **Estrada Parque**, begins halfway between Miranda and Corumbá at a turn-off called Buraco da Piranha (the Piranha hole), heads north into the Pantanal and then, after 51 km, turns west to Corumbá at a point called the Curva do Leque. This is the overland access point to **Nhecolândia** – a region particularly rich in wildlife. Four-wheel drives run by the tour operators or the *fazendeiros* wait at the Buraco da Piranha to meet tour buses arriving from Campo Grande. They then take visitors either to *fazendas* or to campsites in Nhecolândia. *Fazendas* in this area include **Fazenda Rio Negro**, a project run in conjunction with Conservation International and now closed to tourism, **Fazenda Barra Mansa and Fazenda Barranco Alto.** ▸▸ *See page 58.*

Visiting the Northern Pantanal → *For details see Mato Grosso, page 65.*

There are two main access points to the northern Pantanal: the **Transpantaneira road** (see page 67), which cuts through the wetland and is lined with *fazendas*; and the town of **Barão de Melgaço** (see page 68), which is surrounded by large lakes and rivers and is not as good for wildlife. Both are reached from Cuiabá in Mato Grosso.

The Transpantaneira was built in 1976 and was originally planned to connect Cuiabá with Corumbá, but it currently goes only as far as the border at Porto Jofre on the Rio Cuiabá. Work has been suspended indefinitely – ostensibly because of the division of the two Mato Grosso states – and is a superb spot for wildlife watching. Hundreds of thousands of birds congregate here, particularly between June and September, to wade through the shallow wetlands to either side of the road. And at any time of year there seems to be a raptor on every other fence post. Mammals and reptiles can often be spotted crossing the road or even sitting on it, particularly at dawn and dusk. Most of the northern Pantanal's tourist-orientated *fazendas* are here. The road is unpaved, potholed and punctuated by numerous rickety wooden bridges and, although it can be driven in a standard hire car, progress is slow. It is probably better to see the Transpantaneira as part of a tour as most of the guides have access to the *fazendas* along the way. If you choose to go alone, be sure to book in advance; private individuals who turn up unannounced may or may not be welcome at some *fazendas*.

The easiest access is in the dry season (July to September). In the wet, especially January and February, there is no guarantee that you will get all the way to Porto Jofre. Bring plenty of water and some extra fuel as petrol stations often run out. If you choose not to take a tour or hire a car you can hitch a ride along the Transpantaneira from Poconé. Do not travel alone and be prepared for a bumpy ride in the back of a truck. There are several excellent companies based in Cuiabá who offer trips along the Transpantaneira to Porto Jofre, often combining them with visits to the Chapada dos Guimarães (see page 70), Nobres or the Mato Grosso Amazon. They include **Pantanal Nature** and the **Pantanal Bird Club**. ▸ *For further information, see Where to stay, page 76, What to do, page 80, and Transport, page 82.*

Air

Because of the size of the country, flying is often the most practical option and internal air services are highly developed. All state capitals and larger cities are linked with each other with services several times a day, and all national airlines offer excellent service. Recent deregulation of the airlines has greatly reduced prices on some routes and low-cost airlines offer fares that can often be as cheap as travelling by bus (when booked through the internet). Paying with an international credit card is not always possible online; but it is usually possible to buy an online ticket through a hotel, agency or willing friend without surcharge. Many of the smaller airlines go in and out of business sporadically. GOL, Oceanair, TAM, TRIP/Total, Varig, and Webjet operate the most extensive routes. Most of their websites (see below) provide full information, including a booking service, although not all are in English.

Flight schedules are constantly changing and routes frequently close and re-open. Check the airline websites for the latest details and for prices.

Air passes

TAM and GOL offer a 21-day **Brazil Airpass**, which is valid on any TAM destination within Brazil. The price varies according to the number of flights taken and the international airline used to arrive in Brazil. They can only be bought outside Brazil. One to four flights start at around US$540, five flights start at US$680, six flights start at US$840, seven flights start at US$990, eight flights start at US$1120, and nine flights start at US$1259. The baggage allowance is the same as that permitted on their international flights. TAM and Gol also operate as part of the **Mercosur Airpass**, which is valid for Brazil, Argentina, Chile, Uruguay and Paraguay using local carriers. It is valid for any passenger with a return ticket to their country of origin, and must be bought with an international flight. The minimum stay is seven days, maximum 45 and at least two countries must be visited. The maximum number of flights is eight. Fares, worked out on a mileage basis, cost between US$295 and US$1195. Children pay a discounted rate, and under-threes pay 10% of the adult rate. Some of the carriers operate a blackout period between 15 December and 15 January.

Where to stay in the Brazilian Pantanal

There is a good range of accommodation options in Brazil. An *albergue* or hostel offers the cheapest option. These have dorm beds and single and double rooms. Many are part of the **IYHA**, www.iyha.org. **Hostel world**, www.hostelworld.com; **Hostel Bookers**, www.hostel bookers.com; and **Hostel.com**, www.hostel.com, are useful portals. **Hostel Trail Latin America** – T0131-208 0007 (UK), www.hosteltrail.com – managed from their hostel in Popayan, is an online network of hotels and tour companies in South America. A *pensão* is either a cheap guesthouse or a household that rents out some rooms.

A *pousada* is either a bed-and-breakfast, often small and family-run, or a sophisticated and often charming small hotel. A *hotel* is as it is anywhere else in the world, operating according to the international star system, although five-star hotels are not price controlled and hotels in any category are not always of the standard of their star equivalent in the USA, Canada or Europe. Many of the older hotels can be cheaper than hostels. Usually accommodation prices include a breakfast of rolls, ham, cheese, cakes and fruit with coffee and juice; there is no reduction if you don't eat it. Rooms vary too. Normally an *apartamento* is a room with separate living and sleeping areas and sometimes cooking facilities. A *quarto* is a standard room; *com banheiro* is en suite; and *sem banheiro* is with shared bathroom. Finally there are the *motels*. These should not be confused with their US counterpart: motels are used by guests not intending to sleep; there is no stigma attached and they usually offer good value (the rate for a full night is called the '*pernoite*'), however the decor can be a little garish.

It's a good idea to book accommodation in advance in small towns that are popular at weekends with city dwellers (eg near São Paulo and Rio de Janeiro), and it's essential to book at peak times.

Luxury accommodation

Much of the luxury private accommodation sector can be booked through operators. **Angatu**, www.angatu.com, offers the best private homes along the Costa Verde, together with bespoke trips. **Dehouche**, www.dehouche.com, offers upmarket accommodation and trips in Bahia, Rio and Alagoas. **Brazilian Beach House**, www.brazilian beachhouse.com, has

Price codes

Where to stay

$$$$	over US$150
$$$	US$66-150
$$	US$30-65
$	Under US$30

Prices include taxes and service charge, but not meals. They are based on a double room, except in the **$** range, where prices are almost always per person.

Restaurants

$$$	Expensive	over US$20
$$	Mid-range	US$8-20
$	Cheap	under US$8

Prices refer to the cost of a two-course meal, not including drinks.

some of the finest houses in Búzios and Trancoso but is not so great at organizing transfers and pick-ups. **Matuete**, www.matuete.com, has a range of luxurious properties and tours throughout Brazil.

Homestays

Staying with a local family is an excellent way to become integrated quickly into a city and companies try to match guests to their hosts. **Cama e Café**, www.camaecafe.com.br, organizes homestays in Rio de Janeiro, Olinda and a number of other cities around Brazil. **Couch surfing**, www.couchsurfing.com, offers a free, backpacker alternative.

Quality hotel associations

The better international hotel associations have members in Brazil. These include: **Small Luxury Hotels of the World**, www.slh.com; the **Leading Hotels of the World**, www.lhw.com; the **Leading Small Hotels of the World**, www.leadingsmallhotels oftheworld.com; **Great Small Hotels**, www.greatsmallhotels.com; and the **French Relais et Chateaux group**, www.relaischateaux.com, which also includes restaurants.

The Brazilian equivalent of these associations is the **Roteiros de Charme**, www.roteiros decharme.com.br, with some 30 locations in the southeast and northeast. Whilst membership of these groups pretty much guarantees quality, it is by no means comprehensive. There are many fine hotels and charming *pousadas* listed in our text that are not included in these associations.

Online travel agencies (OTAs)

Services like **Tripadvisor** and OTAs associated with them – such as **hotels.com, expedia.com** and **venere.com**, are well worth using for both reviews and for booking ahead. Hotels booked through an OTA can be up to 50% cheaper than the rack rate. Similar sites operate for hostels (though discounts are far less considerable). They include the **Hostelling International** site, www.hihostels.com, **hostelbookers.com, hostels.com** and **hostelworld.com**.

Food and drink in the Brazilian Pantanal

Amazon food

The Amazon has a distinctive range of dishes that make use of the thousands of fruits and vegetables and the abundant fish of the area. Regional food here vies with Bahia as the best in Brazil – especially in Belém, Manaus and Rio Branco. Must-tries include *tacacá*, a soup made with jambo leaves, which numbs the tongue and stimulates energy. The best fish are *pacu* and *tambaqui*, both types of vegetarian piranha (the carnivorous ones can be eaten too). *Jaraqui* is very common in Amazonas – often in a delicious broth. *Pirarucu*, one of the world's largest freshwater fish, is delicious; however, due to overfishing it is in danger of becoming extinct and should only be eaten when sustainably sourced from locations such as Mamirauá. Specialities of Pará state include duck, often served as *pato no tucupi*, in a yellow soup made from the sieved off cassava (manioc) juice and served with *jambo*. *Maniçoba* is made with the poisonous leaves of the *cassava* (bitter manioc), simmered for eight days to get rid of the cyanide. It is jet black but deliciously tangy. *Caldeirada* is a fish and vegetable soup, served with *pirão* (manioc puree), and is a speciality of Amazonas. There is also an enormous variety of tropical and jungle fruits, many unique to the region. Try them fresh, or in ice creams or juices. The best include *tapereba*, *cupuaçu*, *cajú* (the fruit of the cashew nut), *cacau* (the fruit of the cocoa bean) and *camu camu*, which has the highest vitamin C content of any fruit in the world. Avoid food from street vendors, except those selling *tacacá* at the Boi bumba or from **Gisela** in the Praça São Sebastião in Manaus who has been selling delicious *tacacá* for decades, from 1600-2200.

Eating cheaply

The cheapest dish is the *prato feito* or *sortido*, an excellent-value set menu usually comprising meat/chicken/fish, beans, rice, chips and salad. The *prato comercial* is similar but rather better and a bit more expensive. Portions are usually large enough for two and come with two plates. If you are on your own, you could ask for an *embalagem* (doggy bag) or a *marmita* (takeaway) and offer it to a person with no food (many Brazilians do). Many restaurants serve *comida por kilo* buffets where you serve yourself and pay for the weight of food on your plate. This is generally good value and is a good option for vegetarians. *Lanchonetes* and *padarias* (diners and bakeries) are good for cheap eats; usually serving *prato feitos*, *salgadinhos*, excellent juices and other snacks.

The main meal is usually taken in the middle of the day; cheap restaurants tend not to be open in the evening.

Drink

The national liquor is *cachaça* (also known as *pinga*), which is made from sugar-cane, and ranging from cheap supermarket and service-station fire-water, to boutique distillery and connoisseur labels from the interior of Minas Gerais. Mixed with fruit juice, sugar and crushed ice, *cachaça* becomes the principal element in a *batida*, a refreshing but deceptively powerful drink. Served with pulped lime or other fruit, mountains of sugar and smashed ice it becomes the world's favourite party cocktail, caipirinha. A less potent caipirinha made with vodka is called a *caipiroska* and with sake a *saikirinha* or *caipisake*.

Some genuine Scotch whisky brands are bottled in Brazil. They are far cheaper even than duty free; Teacher's is the best. Locally made and cheap gin, vermouth and campari are pretty much as good as their US and European counterparts.

Wine is becoming increasingly popular, with good-value Portuguese and Argentinean bottles and some reasonable national table wines such as Château d'Argent, Château Duvalier, Almadén, Dreher, Preciosa and more respectable Bernard Taillan, Marjolet from Cabernet grapes, and the Moselle-type white Zahringer. A new *adega* tends to start off well, but the quality gradually deteriorates with time; many vintners have switched to American Concorde grapes, producing a rougher wine. Greville Brut champagne-style sparkling wine is inexpensive and very drinkable.

Brazil is the third most important wine producer in South America. The wine industry is mainly concentrated in the south of the country where the conditions are most suitable, with over 90% of wine produced in Rio Grande do Sul. There are some interesting sparkling wines in the Italian spumante style (the best is Casa Valduga Brut Premium Sparkling Wine), and Brazil produces still wines using many international and imported varieties. None are distinguished – these are drinkable table wines at best. At worst they are plonk of the Blue Nun variety. The best bottle of red is probably the Boscato Reserva Cabernet Sauvignon. But it's expensive (at around US$20 a bottle); you'll get far higher quality and better value buying Portuguese, Argentine or Chilean wines in Brazil.

Brazilian beer is generally lager, served ice-cold. Draught beer is called *chope* or *chopp* (after the German Schoppen, and pronounced 'shoppi'). There are various national brands of bottled beers, which include Brahma, Skol, Cerpa, Antartica and the best Itaipava and Bohemia. There are black beers too, notably Xingu. They tend to be sweet. The best beer is from the German breweries in Rio Grande do Sul and is available only there.

Brazil's myriad fruits are used to make fruit juices or *sucos*, which come in a delicious variety, unrivalled anywhere in the world. *Açai, acerola, caju* (cashew), *pitanga, goiaba* (guava), *genipapo, graviola* (chirimoya), *maracujá* (passion fruit), *sapoti, umbu* and *tamarindo* are a few of the best. *Vitaminas* are thick fruit or vegetable drinks with milk. *Caldo de cana* is sugar-cane juice, sometimes mixed with ice. *Água de côco* or *côco verde* is coconut water served straight from a chilled, fresh, green coconut. The best known of many local soft drinks is *guaraná*, which is a very popular carbonated fruit drink, completely unrelated to the Amazon nut. The best variety is *guaraná Antarctica*. Coffee is ubiquitous and good tea entirely absent.

Shopping in the Brazilian Pantanal

Arts and crafts

Brazil does not offer the variety and quality of arts and crafts you'll find in the Andes. However, good buys include: beautiful bead jewellery and bags made from Amazon seeds; clay figurines from the northeast, especially from Pernambuco; lace from Ceará; leatherwork, Marajó pottery and fabric hammocks from Amazônia (be sure to buy hooks – *ganchos para rede* – for hanging your hammock at home); carvings in soapstone and in bone; *capim-dourado* gold-grass bags and jewellery from Tocantins; and African-type pottery, basketwork and *candomblé* artefacts from Bahia. Brazilian cigars are excellent for those who like mild flavours.

How big is your footprint?

→ Where possible choose a destination, tour operator or hotel with a proven ethical and environmental commitment – if in doubt, ask.

→ Spend money on locally produced (rather than imported) goods and services, buy directly from the producer or from a 'fair trade' shop, and use common sense when bargaining – the few dollars you save may be a week's salary to others.

→ Use water and electricity carefully – travellers may receive preferential supply while the needs of local communities are overlooked.

→ Learn about local etiquette and culture – consider local norms and behaviour and dress appropriately for local cultures and situations.

→ Protect wildlife and other natural resources – don't buy souvenirs or goods unless they are sustainably produced and are not protected under CITES legislation.

→ Always ask before taking photographs or videos of people.

→ Consider staying in local accommodation rather than foreign-owned hotels – the economic benefits for host communities are greater – and there are more opportunities to learn about local culture.

→ Within cities, local buses and (in São Paulo) metrôs are fast, cheap and have extensive routes. Try one instead of a taxi, and meet some real Brazilians!

→ Long-distance buses may take longer than flying but they have comfortable reclining seats, some offer drinks, and show up-to-date DVDs. They sometimes have better schedules too.

→ Supermarkets will give you a plastic bag for even the smallest purchases. If you don't need one, let them know – plastic waste is a huge problem – particularly in the northeast. When buying certain drinks, look for the returnable glass bottles.

→ Make a voluntary contribution to Climate Care, www.co2.org, to help counteract the pollution caused by tax-free fuel on your flight.

Festivals in the Brazilian Pantanal

Brazil has festivals all year round with most concentrated in Jun and around Carnaval at the beginning of Lent.

February/March
Carnaval, Brazil's biggest festival takes place throughout the country and most famously in Rio's *sambódromo* stadium. For a wild street party head for Salvador; for something more authentic and traditional, Recife; and for a Brazilian crowd entirely free of foreign tourists, try one of the cities in Brazil's interior such as Cidade de Goiás,

www.vilaboadegoias. com.br/carnaval, or Ouro Preto, www.carnavalouropreto.com.

April
Festa do Açaí, **Festa da Castanha and Festa do Cupuaçu**, Codajás, Tefé and Presidente Figueiredo, Amazonas. 3 festivals devoted to 3 of the best Amazonian foods: the *açaí* energy berry, *cupuaçu* and the Brazil nut.

June
Boi Bumba, Parintins, Amazonas. A huge spectacle re-enacting the Boi story, with 2 competing teams, enormous floats and

troupes of dancers. On an island in the Amazon. See www.boibumba.com.

Bumba-Meu-Boi, São Luís, Maranhão, see www.saoluisturismo.com.br.

Festas Juninas (Festas do São João), Campina Grande, Paraíba, Caruaru, Pernambuco and throughout Brazil. Brazil's major winter festival with hot spiced wine and *forró* dancing.

November

Círio de Nazaré, Belém and throughout Pará and Amazonas states. One of the largest religious celebrations in Brazil. Huge crowds, long precessions and many live music and cultural events. See also ww.paratur.pa.gov.br.

Responsible travel

Sustainable or ecotourism is not just about looking after the physical environment, but also the local community. Whilst it has been slow to catch up with Costa Rica or Ecuador, Brazil now has some first-rate ecotourism projects and the country is a pioneer in urban community tourism in the favelas. Model ecotourism resorts in the forest include **Cristalino Jungle Lodge** (page 79), while **Fazenda San Francisco** in the Pantanal (page 58) runs a pioneering jaguar conservation project. Some state governments cheerfully exploit the colourful local culture while sharing little of the profit. So rather than staying in a big resort and organizing a tour from back home, seek out smaller locally owned hotels and local indigenous guides.

Essentials A-Z

Accident and emergency
Ambulance T192. **Police** T190. If robbed or attacked, contact the tourist police. If you need to claim on insurance, make sure you get a police report.

Electricity
Generally 110 V 60 cycles AC, but in some cities and areas 220 V 60 cycles AC is used. European and U.S 2-pin plugs and sockets.

Embassies and consulates
For embassies and consulates of Brazil, see www.embassiesabroad.com.

Health → *Hospitals/medical services are listed in the Directory sections of each chapter.*
See your GP or travel clinic at least 6 weeks before departure for general advice on travel risks and vaccinations. Try phoning a specialist travel clinic if your own doctor is unfamiliar with health in the region. Make sure you have sufficient medical travel insurance, get a dental check, know your own blood group and, if you suffer a long-term condition such as diabetes or epilepsy, obtain a **Medic Alert** bracelet (www.medicalalert.co.uk).

There is a danger of **malaria** in Amazônia, especially on the brown-water rivers. Mosquito larvae do not breed well in the black-water rivers as they are too acidic. Mosquito nets are not required when in motion as boats travel away from the banks and are too fast for mosquitos to settle. However, nets and repellent can be useful for night stops. Wear long, loose trousers (tight ones are easy to bite through) and a baggy shirt at night and put repellent around shirt collars, cuffs and the tops of socks.
A **yellow fever** inoculation is strongly advised. It is compulsory to have a certificate when crossing borders and those without one will have to get inoculated and wait 10 days before travelling. Other common infections in the Amazon are **dengue**, which is widespread in the Amazon – as it is throughout South America – **cutaneous larva migrans** (a spot that appears to move), which is easily treated with **Thiabendazole**, and **tropical ulcers**, caught by scratching mosquito bites, which then get dirty and become infected. It is advisable to vaccinate against polio, tetanus, typhoid, hepatitis A and, for more remote areas, rabies. Cholera, diptheria and hepatitis B vaccinations are sometimes advised. Specialist advice should be taken on the best antimalarials to take before you leave.

Websites
www.cdc.gov Centres for Disease Control and Prevention (USA).
www.dh.gov.uk/en/Policyandguidance/ Healthadvicefortravellers/index.htm Department of Health advice for travellers.
www.fitfortravel.scot.nhs.uk Fit for Travel (UK), a site from Scotland providing a quick A-Z of vaccine and travel health advice requirements for each country.
www.fco.gov.uk Foreign and Commonwealth Office (FCO), UK.
www.itg.be Prince Leopold Institute for Tropical Medicine.
www.nathnac.org National Travel Health Network and Centre (NaTHNaC).
www.who.int World Health Organisation.

Books
Dawood, R, editor, *Travellers' health*, 3rd ed, Oxford: Oxford University Press, 2002.
Warrell, David, and Sarah Anderson, editors, *Expedition Medicine*, The Royal Geographic Society, ISBN 1 86197 040-4.
Wilson-Howarth, Jane. *Bugs, Bites and Bowels: the essential guide to travel health*, Cadogan 2006.

Internet

Brazil is said to be 7th in the world in terms of internet use. Public internet access is so readily available that it is almost pointless to list the locations. There is internet access on every other street corner in even the smallest towns and cities – look for signs saying '**LAN house**' or '**ciber-café**'. The facilities usually double-up as computer games rooms for teenagers. There is usually an hourly charge of around US$2, but you can almost always use partial hours at a reduced rate. More and more hotels offer an internet service to their guests – many in-room wireless; usually free but sometimes at exorbitant rates, while some government programmes even offer free use (notably in Manaus and Cuiaba) in public areas. For a regularly updated list of locations around the world, check www.netcafe guide.com.

Language

Brazilians speak Portuguese, and very few speak anything else. Spanish may help you to be understood a little, but spoken Portuguese will remain undecipherable even to fluent Spanish speakers. To get the best out of Brazil, learn some Portuguese before arriving. Brazilians are the best thing about the country and without Portuguese you will not be able to interact beyond stereotypes and second guesses. Language classes are available in the larger cities. **Cactus** (www.cactuslanguage.com), **Languages abroad** (www.languages abroad.co.uk) and **Travellers Worldwide** (www.travellersworld wide.com) are among the companies that can organize language courses in Brazil. **McGraw Hill** and **DK** (*Hugo Portuguese in Three Months*) offer the best teach-yourself books. **Sonia Portuguese** (www.sonia- portuguese.com) is a useful online resource.

Money

Currency

➔ *£1 = 3.2; €1 = 2.5; US$1 = R$2 (May 2012).* The unit of currency is the **real**, R$ (plural **reais**). Any amount of foreign currency and 'a reasonable sum' in reais can be taken in, but sums over US$10,000 must be declared. Residents may only take out the equivalent of US$4000. Notes in circulation are: 100, 50, 10, 5 and 1 real; coins: 1 real, 50, 25, 10, 5 and 1 centavo. **Note** The exchange-rate fluctuates – check regularly.

Costs of travelling

Brazil is more expensive than other countries in South America. As a very rough guide, prices are about two-thirds those of Western Europe and a little cheaper than rural USA; though prices vary hugely according to the current exchange rate and strength of the real, whose value has soared since 2008 – with Goldman Sachs and Bloomberg considering the *real* to be the most over-valued major currency in the world in 2009-2010. It is expected to lose value; check on the latest before leaving on currency exchange sites such as www.x-rates.com.

Hostel beds are usually around US$15. Budget hotels with few frills have rooms for as little as US$30, and you should have no difficulty finding a double room costing US$45 wherever you are. Rooms are often pretty much the same price whether 1 or 2 people are staying. Eating is generally inexpensive, especially in *padarias* or *comida por kilo* (pay by weight) restaurants, which offer a wide range of food (salads, meat, pasta, vegetarian). Expect to pay around US$6 to eat your fill in a good-value restaurant. Although bus travel is cheap by US or European standards, because of the long distances, costs can soon mount up. Internal flights prices have come down dramatically in the last couple of years and some routes work out cheaper than taking a bus – especially if booking through the internet. Prices vary regionally. Ipanema is almost twice as expensive as rural Bahia. A can of beer in a supermarket in the southeast costs US$0.80, a litre of water US$0.60, a single metrô ticket in São Paulo US$1.60, a bus ticket between US$1 and US$1.50 (depending on the city) and a cinema ticket around US$3.60.

ATMs

ATMs, or cash machines, are common in Brazil. As well as being the most convenient way of withdrawing money, they frequently offer the best available rates of exchange. They are usually closed after 2130 in large cities. There are 2 international ATM acceptance systems, **Plus** and **Cirrus**. Many issuers of debit and credit cards are linked to one, or both (eg Visa is Plus, MasterCard is Cirrus). **Bradesco** and **HSBC** are the 2 main banks offering this service. **Red Banco 24 Horas** kiosks advertise that they take a long list of credit cards in their ATMs, including MasterCard and Amex, but international cards cannot always be used; the same is true of **Banco do Brasil**.

There are plenty of ATM facilities in all the Amazon's main towns (the state capitals, Santarém, Cruzeiro do Sul, Marabá, Parintins and São Gabriel da Cachoeira), where there is an **HSBC**, **Bradesco** or **Banco 24 horas**. Small amounts of US dollars cash can usually be exchanged away from banks at a poor rate, but are not accepted as local currency. The rate of exchange for TCs is appalling.

Advise your bank before leaving, as cards are usually stopped in Brazil without prior warning. Find out before you leave what international functionality your card has. Check if your bank or credit card company imposes handling charges. Internet banking is useful for monitoring your account or transferring funds. Do not rely on 1 card, in case of loss. If you do lose a card, immediately contact the 24-hr helpline of the issuer in your home country (keep this number in a safe place).

Exchange

Banks in major cities will change cash and traveller's cheques (TCs), but the rate of exchange for traveller's cheques is appalling. If you keep the official exchange slips, you may convert back into foreign currency up to 50% of the amount you exchanged. The parallel market, found in travel agencies, exchange houses and among hotel staff, often offers marginally better rates than the banks but commissions can be very high. Many banks may only change US$300 minimum in cash, US$500 in TCs. Rates for TCs are usually far lower than for cash, they are harder to change and a very heavy commission may be charged. Dollars cash (take US$5 or US$10 bills) are not useful as alternative currency. Brazilians use *reais*.

Credit cards

Credit cards are widely used, athough often they are not usable in the most unlikely of places, such as tour operators. **Diners Club**, **MasterCard**, **Visa** and **Amex** are useful. Cash advances on credit cards will only be paid in *reais* at the tourist rate, incurring at least a 1.5% commission. Banks in small, remote places may still refuse to give a cash advance: try asking for the *gerente* (manager).

Money transfers

Money sent to Brazil is normally paid out in Brazilian currency, so do not have more money sent out than you need for your stay. Funds can ostensibly be received within 48 banking hours, but it can take at least a month to arrive, allowing banks to capitalize on your transfer. The documentation required to receive it varies according to the whim of the bank staff, making the whole procedure often far more trouble than it is worth.

Opening hours

Generally Mon-Fri 0900-1800; closed for lunch some time between 1130 and 1400.

Shops Also open on Sat until 1230 or 1300.
Government offices Mon-Fri 1100-1800.
Banks Mon-Fri 1000-1600 or 1630;
closed at weekends.

Safety

Although Brazil's big cities suffer high rates of violent crime, this is mostly confined to the favelas (slums) where poverty and drugs are the main cause. Visitors should not enter favelas except when accompanied by workers for NGOs, tour groups or other people who know the local residents well and are accepted by the community. Otherwise they may be targets of muggings by armed gangs who show short shrift to those who resist them. Mugging can take place anywhere. Travel light after dark with few valuables (avoid wearing jewellery and use a cheap, plastic, digital watch). Ask hotel staff where is and isn't safe; crime is patchy in Brazilian cities.

If the worst does happen and you are threatened, don't panic, and hand over your valuables. Do not resist, and report the crime to the local tourist police later. It is extremely rare for a tourist to be hurt during a robbery in Brazil. Being aware of the dangers, acting confidently and using your common sense will reduce many of the risks.

Photocopy your passport, air ticket and other documents, make a record of traveller's cheque and credit card numbers. Keep them separately from the originals and leave another set of records at home. Keep all documents secure; hide your main cash supply in different places or under your clothes. Extra pockets sewn inside shirts and trousers, money belts (best worn below the waist), neck or leg pouches and elasticated support bandages for keeping money above the elbow or below the knee have been repeatedly recommended.

All border areas should be regarded with some caution because of smuggling activities. Violence over land ownership

in parts of the interior have resulted in a 'Wild West' atmosphere in some towns, which should therefore be passed through quickly. Red-light districts should also be given a wide berth as there are reports of drinks being drugged with a substance popularly known as 'good night Cinderella'. This leaves the victim easily amenable to having their possessions stolen, or worse.

Avoiding cons

Never trust anyone telling sob stories or offering 'safe rooms', and when looking for a hotel, always choose the room yourself. Be wary of 'plain-clothes policemen'; insist on seeing identification and on going to the police station by main roads. Do not hand over your identification (or money) until you are at the station. On no account take them directly back to your hotel. Be even more suspicious if they seek confirmation of their status from a passer-by.

Hotel security

Hotel safe deposits are generally, but not always, secure. If you cannot get a receipt for valuables in a hotel safe, you can seal the contents in a plastic bag and sign across the seal. Always keep an inventory of what you have deposited. If you don't trust the hotel, lock everything in your pack and secure it in your room when you go out. If you lose valuables, report to the police and note details of the report for insurance purposes. Be sure to be present whenever your credit card is used.

Police

There are several types of police: **Polícia Federal**, civilian dressed, who handle all federal law duties, including immigration. A subdivision is the **Polícia Federal Rodoviária**, uniformed, who are the traffic police on federal highways. **Polícia Militar** are the uniformed, street police force, under the control of the state governor, handling all state laws. They are not the same as the

Armed Forces' internal police. **Política Civil**, also state controlled, handle local laws and investigations. They are usually in civilian dress, unless in the traffic division. In cities, the **Prefeitura** controls the **Guarda Municipal**, who handle security. **Tourist police** operate in places with a strong tourist presence. In case of difficulty, visitors should seek out tourist police in the first instance.

Public transport
When you have all your luggage with you at a bus or railway station, be especially careful and carry any shoulder bags in front of you. To be extra safe, take a taxi between the airport/bus station/railway station and hotel, keep your bags with you and pay only when you and your luggage are outside; avoid night buses and arriving at your destination at night.

Women travellers
Most of these tips apply to any single traveller. When you set out, err on the side of caution until your instincts have adjusted to the customs of a new culture. Be prepared for the exceptional curiosity extended to visitors, especially women, and try not to overreact. If, as a single woman, you can befriend a local woman, you will learn much more about the country you are visiting. There is a definite 'gringo trail' you can follow, which can be helpful when looking for safe accommodation, especially if arriving after dark (best avoided). Remember that for a single woman a taxi at night can be as dangerous as walking alone. It is easier for men to take the friendliness of locals at face value; women may be subject to unwanted attention. Do not disclose to strangers where you are staying. By wearing a wedding ring and saying that your 'husband' is close at hand, you may dissuade an aspiring suitor. If politeness fails, do not feel bad about showing offence and departing. A good rule is always to act with confidence, as though you know where you are going, even if you do not.

Someone who looks lost is more likely to attract unwanted attention.

Tax
Airport departure tax The amount of tax depends on the class and size of the airport, but the cost is usually incorporated into the ticket.
VAT Rates vary from 7-25% at state and federal level; the average is 17-20%.

Telephone
→ *Country code: +55.*
Ringing: equal tones with long pauses. Engaged: equal tones, equal pauses.

Making a phone call in Brazil can be confusing. It is necessary to dial a 2-digit telephone company code prior to the area code for all calls. Phone numbers are now printed in this way: 0XX21 (0 for a national call, XX for the code of the phone company chosen (eg 31 for Telemar) followed by, 21 for Rio de Janeiro, for example and the 8-digit number of the subscriber. The same is true for international calls where 00 is followed by the operator code and then the country code and number.

Telephone operators and their codes are: **Embratel**, 21 (nationwide); **Telefônica**, 15 (state of São Paulo); **Telemar**, 31 (Alagoas, Amazonas, Amapá, Bahia, Ceará, Espírito Santo, Maranhão, most of Minas Gerais, Pará, Paraíba, Pernambuco, Piauí, Rio de Janeiro, Rio Grande do Norte, Roraima, Sergipe); **Tele Centro-Sul**, 14 (Acre, Goiás, Mato Grosso, Mato Grosso do Sul, Paraná, Rondônia, Santa Catarina, Tocantins and the cities of Brasília and Pelotas); **CTBC-Telecom**, 12 (some parts of Minas Gerais, Goiás, Mato Grosso do Sul and São Paulo state); **Intelig**, 23.

National calls
Telephone booths or *orelhões* (literally 'big ears' as they are usually ear-shaped, fibreglass shells) are easy to come by in

towns and cities. Local phone calls and telegrams are cheap.

Cartões telefônicos (phone cards) are available from newsstands, post offices and some chemists. They cost US$4 for 30 units and up to US$7 for 90 units. Local calls from a private phone are often free. *Cartões telefônicos internacionais* (international phone cards) are increasingly available in tourist areas and are often sold at hostels.

Mobile phones

Cellular phones are widespread and coverage excellent even in remote areas, but prices are extraordinarily high and users still pay to receive calls outside the metropolitan area where their phone is registered. SIM cards are hard to buy as users require a CPF (a Brazilian social security number) to buy one, but phones can be hired. When using a cellular telephone you do not drop the zero from the area code as you have to when dialling from a fixed line.

Time

Brazil has 4 time zones: Brazilian standard time is GMT-3; the Amazon time zone (Pará west of the Rio Xingu, Amazonas, Roraima, Rondônia, Mato Grosso and Mato Grosso do Sul) is GMT-4, the State of Acre is GMT-5; and the Fernando de Noronha archipelago is GMT-2. Clocks move forward 1 hr in summer for approximately 5 months (usually between Oct and Feb or Mar), but times of change vary. This does not apply to Acre.

Tipping

Tipping is not usual, but always appreciated as staff are often paid a pittance. In restaurants, add 10% of the bill if no service charge is included; cloakroom attendants deserve a small tip; porters have fixed charges but often receive tips as well; unofficial car parkers on city streets should be tipped 2 reais.

Tour operators

UK

Austral Tours, 20 Upper Tachbrook St, London SW1V 1SH, T020-7233 5384, www.latinamerica.co.uk. Tours to Rio, the Amazon and the northeast.

Condor Journeys and Adventures, 2 Ferry Bank, Colintraive, Argyll PA22 3AR, T01700-841 318, www.condorjourneys-adventures.com. Tailor-made journeys to standard destinations.

Explore Worldwide, 1 Frederick St, Aldershot, Hants GU11 1LQ, T01252-760 000, www.exploreworldwide.com. Standard small-group trips to the northeast, Amazon and Rio.

Journey Latin America, 12-13 Heathfield Terr, Chiswick, London W4 4JE, T020-8747 8315, www.journeylatinamerica.co.uk. Long-established company with excellent escorted tours to some interesting areas like Goiás and the Chapada Diamantina. They also offer a wide range of good-value flight options.

Last Frontiers, The Mill, Quainton Rd, Waddesdon, Bucks HP18 0LP, T01296-653000, www.lastfrontiers.com. Imaginative tailor-made tours to some interesting out-of-the-way locations including Fernando de Noronha.

Select Latin America, 3.51 Canterbury Court, 1-3 Brixton Rd, Kennington Park Business Centre, London SW9 6DE, T020-7407 1478, www.selectlatin america.co.uk. Quality tailor-made holidays and small group tours.

Songlines Music Travel, T020-8505 2582, www.songlines.co.uk/musictravel . Specialist Carnaval packages in Bahia and São Paulo with a break on the beach afterwards. Tour guides offer the chance to meet many of the musicians and to hear the best live music as well as attend the key Carnaval shows.

Steppes Latin America, 51 Castle St, Cirencester, Glos GL7 1QD, T01285-885333, www.steppestravel.co.uk.

Tailor-made and group itineraries throughout Brazil and Latin America.

Sunvil Latin America, Sunvil House, Upper Square, Old Isleworth, Middlesex TW7 7BJ, T020-8568 4499, www.sunvil.co.uk. A good range of options throughout Brazil, including some out-of-the-way destinations.

Tell Tale Travel, 25a Kensington Church St, 1st floor, London, T0800-011 2571; www.telltaletravel.co.uk. Imaginative and well-researched bespoke holidays throughout Brazil, with homestays and light adventure trips aiming to integrate locals and visitors and show Brazil from a Brazilian perspective.

Trips Worldwide, 14 Frederick Place, Clifton, Bristol BS8 1AS, T0117-311 4400, www.tripsworldwide.co.uk. Tailor-made trips throughout South America.

Veloso Tours, ground floor, 34 Warple Way, London W3 0RG, T020-8762 0616, www.veloso.com. An imaginative range of tours throughout Brazil and bespoke options on request.

Wildlife and birding specialists

Naturetrek, Cheriton Mill, Cheriton, Alresford, Hants SO24 0NG, T01962-733051; www.nature trek.co.uk. Wildlife tours throughout Brazil with bespoke options and specialist birding tours of the Atlantic coastal rainforests.

Ornitholidays, 29 Straight Mile, Romsey, Hants SO51 9BB, T01794-519445, www.ornit holidays.co.uk. Annual or biannual birding trips throughout Brazil; usually to the Pantanal, Atlantic Coast rainforest and Iguaçu.

Reef and Rainforest Tours Ltd, A7 Dart Marine Park, Steamer Quay, Totnes, Devon, TQ9 5DR, T01803-866965, www.reefandrainforest.co.uk. Specialists in tailor-made and group wildlife tours.

Wildlife World Wide, Long Barn South, Sutton Manor Farm, Bishop's Sutton, Alresford, Hants SO24 0AA, www.wildlife worldwide.com. Wildlife trips to the Amazon

(on board the Amazon Clipper), Pantanal, safaris on the Transpantaneira and Iguaçu; with bespoke options available.

Wildwings, 577-579 Fishponds Rd, Fishponds, Bristol BS16 3AF, T0117-965 8333, www.wildwings.co.uk. Jaguar tours around Porto Jofre in the Pantanal with extensions to the Atlantic coastal rainforests and elsewhere.

North America

4starSouth America, T1-800-887 5686, www.4starSouthAmerica.com. Customized or scheduled tours throughout South America. Also has an office in Brazil at Av NS Copacabana 1066/907, Rio de Janeiro, T021-2267 6624.

Brazil For Less, /201 Wood Hollow Dr, Austin, TX 78731, T1-877-565 8119 (US toll free) or T+44-203-006 2507 (UK), www.brazilforless.com. US-based travel firm with a focus solely on South America, with local offices and operations, and a price guarantee. Good-value tours, run by travellers for travellers. Will meet or beat any published rates on the internet from outside Brazil.

Ela Brasil Tours, 14 Burlington Dr, Norwalk, CT 06851, T203-840 9010, www.elabrasil.com. Excellent bespoke tours throughout Brazil to some very imaginative destinations. Uses only the best and most responsible local operators.

Ladatco Tours, 3006 Aviation Av 4C, Coconut Grove, Florida 33133, USA, T1800-327 6162, www.ladatco.com. Standard tours to Rio, Iguaçu and Manaus for the Amazon.

Mila Tours, 100 S Greenleaf Av, Gurnee, IL 60031-337, T847-248 2111, T800-387 7378 (USA and Canada), www.milatours.com. Itineraries to Rio, Iguaçu and the northeast.

Wildlife and birding specialists

Birding Brazil, www.birdingbrazil.com. Richard Raby is one of the only US operators taking wildlife and birdwatchers to Bahia.

Field Guides, 9433 Bee Cave Rd, Building 1, Suite 150, Austin, Texas 78733, USA, T1-800-

7284953, www.fieldguides.com. Interesting birdwatching tours to all parts of Brazil.

Focus Tours, PO Box 22276, Santa Fe, NM 87502; T(505)216 7780; www.focustours. com. Environmentally responsible travel throughout Brazil with some tour options including parts of Bahia.

Tropical Nature Travel, PO Box 5276, Gainesville, Fl 326270 5276, USA, T352-376 3377, www.tropicalnaturetravel.com. Ecotourism tours to *fazendas* in the northern and southern Pantanal, **Cristalino Jungle Lodge**, the Amazon (with Amazon Clipper), Iguaçu and the Mata Atlântica.

Brazil

Ambiental, Av Brigadeiro Faria Lima 156, Pinheiros, São Paulo, T011-3818 4600, www.ambiental.tur.br. Trips to every corner of Brazil from Jalapão and Fernando de Noronha to the Pantanal and Iguaçu.

Brazil Always Summer, SEPS EQ 714/914, Bloco E, Sala 409, Edifício Talento, Brasilia-DF, CEP 70390-145, T061-3039 4442, www.brazilalwayssummer.com. Tour operator specializing in holidays to Brazil. Services include hotel booking, Rio Carnaval tickets and excellent car rental rates. English-speaking staff.

Brazil Nature Tours, R Guia Lopes 150, 1st floor, Campo Grande, MS, T067-3042 4659, www.brazilnaturetours.com. Booking agents for nature-based tours to the Pantanal and the Amazon.

Cariri Ecotours, R Francisco Gurgel, 9067, Ponta Negra Beach, Natal, T084-9928 0198, www.caririecotours.com.br. If ecotourism means wildlife then Manary are not eco at all, but they do offer unusual, exciting tours to the northeastern *sertão*, including the spectacular Serra da Capivara (to see the rock paintings), Cariri and the fossilized dinosaur prints in Paraíba. Very professional service.

Dehouche, T021-2512 3895, www.dehouche.com. Upmarket, carefully tailored trips throughout Brazil.

Matueté, T011-3071 4515, www.matuete. com. Bespoke luxury options around Brazil including a range of private house rentals.

Tatur Turismo, Av Tancredo Neves 274, Centro Empresarial Iguatemi, Sala 228, Bloco B, Salvador, 41820-020, Bahia, T071-3114 7900, www.tatur.com.br. Very helpful and professional bespoke Bahia-based agency who can organize tours throughout Brazil, especially in Bahia, using many of the smaller hotels.

whl.travel, T031-3889 8596, www.whlbrazil. com. Online network of tour operators for booking accommodation and tours throughout Brazil.

Wildlife and birding specialists
Andy and Nadime Whittaker's Birding Brazil Tours, www.birdingbraziltours.com. Another good company, based in Manaus. The couple worked with the BBC Natural History Unit on David Attenborough's *The Life of Birds* and are ground agents for a number of the major birding tour companies from the US and Europe.

Birding Brazil Tours, www.birdingbrazil tours.com. Bespoke options only.

Ciro Albano, www.nebrazilbirding.com. The best operator for the northeast of Brazil offering the broadest spread of Bahian birding and wildlife sites, including Estação Veracruz, Canudos and the Chapada Diamantina.

Edson Endrigo, www.avesfoto.com.br. Bespoke options only.

Tourist information
The **Ministério do Turismo**, Esplanada dos Ministérios, Bloco U, 2nd and 3rd floors, Brasília, www.turismo.gov.br or www.braziltour.com, is in charge of tourism in Brazil and has information in many languages. **Embratur**, the Brazilian Institute of Tourism, is at the same address, and is in charge of promoting tourism abroad. For information and phone numbers for your country visit www.braziltour.com. Local

tourist information bureaux are not usually helpful for information on cheap hotels – they generally just dish out pamphlets. Expensive hotels provide tourist magazines for their guests. Telephone directories (not Rio) contain good street maps.

Useful websites

www.amcham.com.br American Chamber of Commerce in São Paulo. A good source of information on local markets.

www.brazil.org.uk Provides a broad range of info on Brazilian history and culture from the UK Brazilian embassy.

www.brazil4you.com Comprehensive travel and tourism info on everything from sights to hotels and weather.

www.brazilmax.com Excellent information on culture and lifestyle, the best available in English.

www.braziltourism.org The official tourism website of Brazil, and the best.

www.gringos.com.br An excellent source of information on all things Brazilian for visitors and expats.

www.ipanema.com A quirky, informative site on all things Rio de Janeiro.

www.maria-brazil.org A wonderfully personal introduction to Brazil, specifically Rio, featuring Maria's cookbook and little black book, features and reviews.

www.rainforestweb.org Excellent, accurate information on rainforest-related issues with detailed comprehensive information on Brazil and extensive links.

http://redebma.ning.com/ By far the best site on Brazilian music with countless profiles of genres, musicians and bands and excellent links.

www.socioambiental.org Invaluable for up-to-the-minute, accurate information on environmental and indigenous issues.

www.survival-international.org The world's leading campaign organization for

indigenous peoples with excellent info on various Brazilian indigenous groups.

www.worldtwitch.com Birding information and comprehensive listings of rainforest lodges.

Visas and immigration

Visas are not required for stays of up to 90 days by tourists from Andorra, Argentina, Austria, Bahamas, Barbados, Belgium, Bolivia, Chile, Colombia, Costa Rica, Denmark, Ecuador, Finland, France, Germany, Greece, Iceland, Ireland, Italy, Liechtenstein, Luxembourg, Malaysia, Monaco, Morocco, Namibia, the Netherlands, Norway, Paraguay, Peru, Philippines, Portugal, San Marino, South Africa, Spain, Suriname, Sweden, Switzerland, Thailand, Trinidad and Tobago, United Kingdom, Uruguay, the Vatican and Venezuela. For them, only the following documents are required at the port of disembarkation: a passport valid for at least 6 months (or *cédula de identidad* for nationals of Argentina, Chile, Paraguay and Uruguay); and a return or onward ticket, or adequate proof that you can purchase your return fare, subject to no remuneration being received in Brazil and no legally binding or contractual documents being signed. Venezuelan passport holders can stay for 60 days on filling in a form at the border.

Citizens of the USA, Canada, Australia, New Zealand and other countries not mentioned above, and anyone wanting to stay longer than 180 days, *must* get a visa before arrival, which may, if you ask, be granted for multiple entry. US citizens must be fingerprinted on entry to Brazil. Visa fees vary from country to country, so apply to the Brazilian consulate in your home country. The consular fee in the USA is US$55. Students planning to study in Brazil or employees of foreign companies can apply for a 1- or 2-year visa. 2 copies of the application form, 2 photos, a letter from the sponsoring company or educational institution in Brazil, a police form showing no criminal convictions and a fee of around US$80 is required.

Identification

You must always carry identification when in Brazil. Take a photocopy of the personal details in your passport, plus your Brazilian immigration stamp, and leave your passport in the hotel safe deposit. This photocopy, when authorized in a *cartório*, US$1, is a legitimate copy of your documents. Be prepared, however, to present the originals when travelling in sensitive border areas. Always keep an independent record of your passport details. Also register with your consulate to expedite document replacement if yours gets lost or stolen.

Warning Do not lose the entry/exit permit they give you when you enter Brazil. Leaving the country without it, you may have to pay up to US$100 per person. It is suggested that you photocopy this form and have it authenticated at a *cartório*, US$1, in case of loss or theft.

Weights and measures
Metric.

Working in Brazil

Volunteering
The **Task Brasil Trust**, T020-7735 5545, www.taskbrasil.org.uk, is a small UK-based charity set up to help abandoned street children in Brazil. It runs various projects to improve the lives of children and pregnant teenage girls, especially those living on the streets of Rio de Janeiro. You can get involved as a volunteer in Brazil, to help the children with sports, reading and writing, music, art and computer skills. Volunteer at the UK or US offices, or make a donation.

Contents

São Paulo

São Paulo

The city of São Paulo is vast and can feel intimidating at first. But this is a city of separate neighbourhoods, only a few of which are interesting for visitors and, once you have your base, it is easy to negotiate. Those who don't flinch from the city's size and who are prepared to spend money and time here, and who get to know Paulistanos, are seldom disappointed. (The inhabitants of the city are called Paulistanos, to differentiate them from the inhabitants of the state, who are called Paulistas.) Nowhere in Brazil is better for concerts, clubs, theatre, ballet, classical music, all round nightlife, restaurants and beautifully designed hotels.

Arriving in São Paulo → *Phone code: 011.*

Getting there There are air services from all parts of Brazil, Europe, North and South America to the international **airport** at Guarulhos, also known as Cumbica, Avenida Monteiro Lobato 1985, T2445 2945 (30 km northeast of the city). The local airport of Congonhas, 14 km south of the city centre on Avenida Washington Luiz, is used for the Rio-São Paulo shuttle. It receives some flights to Belo Horizonte and Vitória and private flights only, T5090 9000. The **main rodoviária** is Tietê (T2223 7152), which is very convenient and has its own Metrô station. There are three other bus stations for inter-state bus services. ▸▸ *See also Transport, page 37.*

Getting around and orientation Much of the centre is pedestrianized, so walking is the only option if you wish to explore it. The best and cheapest way to get around São Paulo is on the Metrô system, which is clean, safe, cheap and efficient, and eing expanded. Bus routes can be confusing and slow due to frequent traffic jams, but buses are safe, clean and only crowded at peak hours. All the rodoviárias (bus stations) are on the Metrô, but if travelling with luggage, take a taxi. The **Old Centre** (Praça da República, Sé, Santa Cecília) is a place to visit but not to stay. The central commercial district, containing banks, offices and shops, is known as the Triângulo, bounded by Ruas Direita, 15 (Quinze) de Novembro, São Bento and Praça Antônio Prado, but it is rapidly spreading towards the Praça da República. **Jardins**, the city's most affluent inner neighbourhood, is a good place to stay and to visit, especially if you want to shop and eat well. Elegant little streets hide hundreds of wonderful restaurants and accommodation ranges from the luxurious to the top end of the budget range. You are safe here at night. The northeastern section of Jardins, known as **Cerqueira César**, abuts one of São Paulo's grandest modern avenues, **Paulista**, lined with skyscrapers, shops and a few churches and museums including MASP (Museu de Arte de São Paulo). There are metro connections from here and a number of good hotels. **Ibirapuera Park and around**: the inner city's largest green space is home to a handful of museums, running tracks, a lake and frequent free live concerts on Sun. The adjoining neighbourhoods of Moema and Vila Mariana have a few hotels, but **Moema, Itaim** and **Vila Olimpia** are among the nightlife centres of São Paulo with a wealth of streetside bars, designer restaurants and European-style dance clubs. Hotels tend to be expensive as they are near the new business centre on Avenidas Brigadeiro Faria Lima and Luis Carlos Berrini. **Pinheiros and Vila Madalena** are less chic, but equally lively at night and with the funkiest shops.

Beware of assaults and pickpocketing in São Paulo. Thieves often use the mustard-on-the-back trick to distract you while someone else robs you. The areas around Luz station, Praça da República and Centro are not safe at night, and do not enter favelas.

Tourist offices There are tourist information booths with English speaking staff in arrivals of terminals 1 and 2 at Guarulhos airport (Cumbica, 0600-2200); and tourist booths in the Tietê bus station (0600-2200) and in the following locations throughout the city: **Olido** ① *Av São João 473, Mon-Fri 0900-1800*; at Parque Prefeito Mário Covas ① *Av Paulista 1853, daily 0800-2000*; at the Mercado Municipal ① *R da Cantareira 306, Mon-Sat 0900-1800, Sun 0700-1600*. An excellent map is available free at all these offices, as well as free maps and pamphlets in English. Visit www.cidadedesaopaulo.com (Portuguese, English and Spanish), also www.guiasp.com.br for what's on and where to go. Editora Abril also publish maps and an excellent guide, *Guia de São Paolo - Sampa* (Portuguese), see www.abril.com.br.

Climate São Paulo sits on a plateau at around 800 m and the weather is temperamental. Rainfall is ample and temperatures fluctuate greatly: summer averages 20-30°C (occasionally peaking into the high 30s or 40s), winter temperatures are 15-25°C (occasionally dropping to below 10° C). The winter months (April-October) are also the driest, with minimal precipitation in June/July. Christmas and New Year are wet. When there are thermal inversions, air pollution can be troublesome.

Centro Histórico

A focal point of the centre is the **Parque Anhangabaú**, an open space between the Triângulo and the streets which lead to Praça da República (Metrô Anhangabaú is at its southern end). Beneath Anhangabaú, north-south traffic is carried by a tunnel. Crossing it are two viaducts: **Viaduto do Chá**, which is open to traffic and links Rua Direita and Rua Barão de Itapetininga. Along its length sellers of potions, cures, fortunes and trinkets set up their booths. The **Viaduto Santa Ifigênia**, an iron bridge for pedestrians only, connects Largo de São Bento with Largo de Santa Ifigênia.

On **Largo de São Bento** there is the **Igreja e Mosteiro de São Bento** ① *T3328 8799, www.mosteiro.org.br for details of all services, including Gregorian chant*, an early 20th-century building (1910-22) on the site of a 1598 chapel. Due south of São Bento is the **Martinelli building** ① *on R Líbero Badaró at Av São João, closed*, the city's first skyscraper (1922). It was surpassed by the **Edifício Banespa** (finished 1947) ① *R João Brícola 24, T3249 7180, Mon-Fri 1000-1700, US$4*, with 360° views from the top, up to 40 km, smog permitting. The renovated **Pateo do Collégio (Museu de Anchieta)** ① *Praça Pátio do Colégio, T3105 6899, www.pateodocollegio. com.br, Metrô Sé, with a café, Tue-Sun 0900-1700, US$3*. It is an exact replica of the original Jesuit church and college but dates from

① São Paulo

São Paulo maps

Where to stay 🛏

1 Blue Tree Towers E3
2 Casa Club C2
3 Formule 1 Paraíso D5
4 Global Hostel D5
5 Grand Hyatt E2
6 Hilton E2
7 Praça da Árvore Hostel E5
8 Sampa Hostel C2
9 Vergueiro Hostel C5

Bars & clubs ♪

1 A Marcenaria C2
2 Bambu C2
3 Genial C2
4 Grazie a Dio C2
5 Ó de Borogodó C2
6 Posto 6 C2

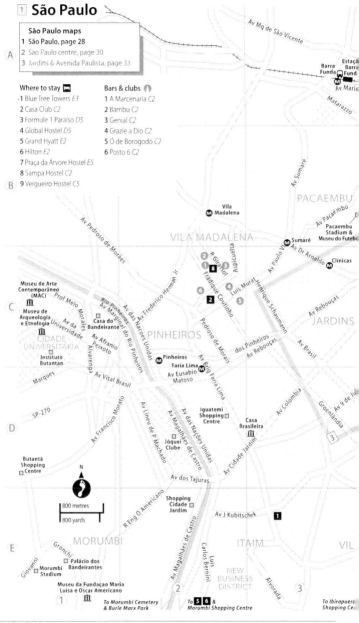

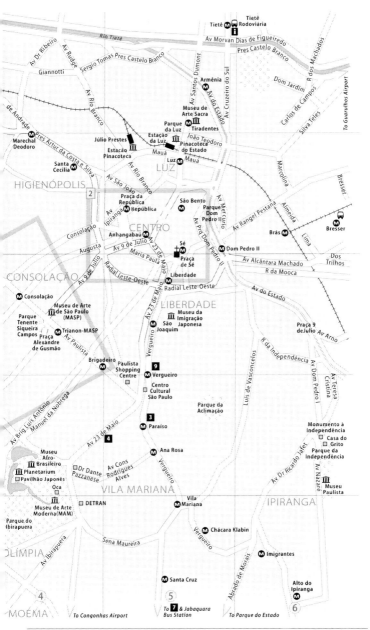

1950s. Most of the buildings are occupied by the Museu de Anchieta, named after the Jesuit captain who led the first mission. This houses, amongst other items a 17th-century font that was used to baptize *indígenas* and a collection of Guaraní art and artefacts from the colonial era and a modernist painting of the priest, by Italian Albino Menghini.

A short distance southeast of the Pateo do Collégio is the **Solar da Marquesa de Santos**, an 18th-century residential building, which now contains the **Museu da Cidade** ⓘ *R Roberto Simonsen 136, T3241 1081, www.museudacidade.sp.gov.br, Tue-Sun 0900-1700.* The **Praça da Sé** is a huge open area south of the Pateo do Collégio, dominated by the **Catedral Metropolitana** ⓘ *T3107 6832, Mon-Sat 0800-1700, Sun 0800-1830,* a massive, peaceful space. The cathedral's foundations were laid more than

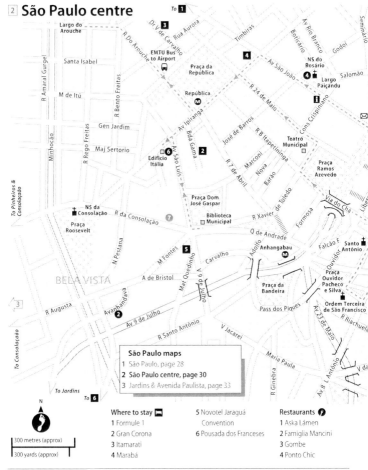

2 São Paulo centre

São Paulo maps
1 São Paulo, page 28
2 São Paulo centre, page 30
3 Jardins & Avenida Paulista, page 33

Where to stay 🛏
1 Formule 1
2 Gran Corona
3 Itamarati
4 Marabá
5 Novotel Jaraguá Convention
6 Pousada dos Franceses

Restaurants 🍴
1 Aska Lámen
2 Famiglia Mancini
3 Gombe
4 Ponto Chic

N
300 metres (approx)
300 yards (approx)

40 years before its inauguration during the 1954 festivities commemorating the fourth centenary of the city. It was fully completed in 1970. This enormous building in neo-Gothic style has a capacity for 8000 worshippers in its five naves. The interior is mostly unadorned, except for the two gilt mosaic pictures in the transepts: on the north side is the Virgin Mary and on the south Saint Paul.

West of the Praça da Sé, along Rua Benjamin Constant, is the Largo de São Francisco. Here is the **Igreja da Ordem Terceira de São Francisco** ⓘ *T3105 6899, 0730-2000*. The convent was inaugurated in 1647 and reformed in 1744. To the right is the Igreja das Chagas do Seráphico Pai São Francisco (1787), painted like its neighbour in blue and gold. Across the Viaduto do Chá is the **Teatro Municipal** ⓘ *T3223 3022*, one of the few distinguished early 20th- century survivors that São Paulo can boast. Viewing the interior may only be possible during a performance; as well as the full evening performances, look out for its midday, string quartet and 'vesperais líricas' concerts.

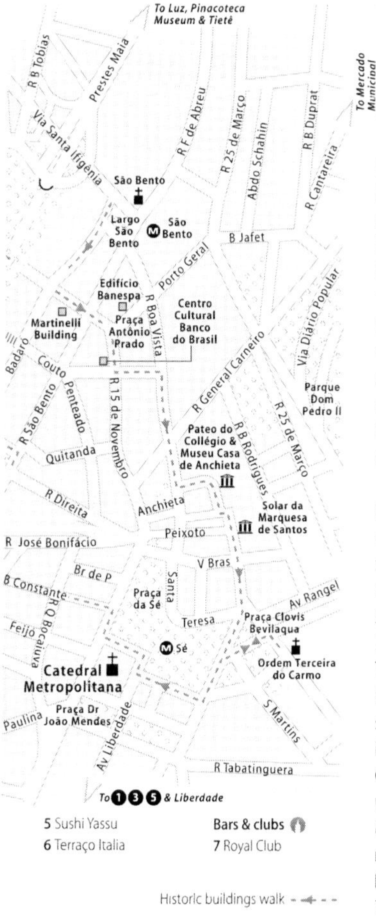
To Luz, Pinacoteca Museum & Tietê
To Mercado Municipal
R B Tobias
Prestes Maia
Via Santa Ifigênia
R F de Abreu
R 25 de Março
Abdo Schahin
R B Duprat
R Cantareira
São Bento
Largo São Bento
São Bento
B Jafet
Porto Geral
Edifício Banespa
Centro Cultural Banco do Brasil
Martinelli Building
Praça Antônio Prado
R Boa Vista
Via Diário Popular
R General Carneiro
Badaró
Couto
Penteado
R São Bento
R 15 de Novembro
Parque Dom Pedro II
R 25 de Março
Pateo do Collégio & Museu Casa de Anchieta
R B Rodrigues
Quitanda
R Direita
Anchieta
Solar da Marquesa de Santos
Peixoto
R José Bonifácio
V Bras
Br de P
B Constante
Praça da Sé
Santa
Av Rangel
R Q Bocaiuva
Feijó
Teresa
Praça Clovis Bevilaqua
Sé
Ordem Terceira do Carmo
Catedral Metropolitana
Praça Dr João Mendes
Paulina
Av Liberdade
S Martins
R Tabatinguera
To 1 3 5 & Liberdade
5 Sushi Yassu
6 Terraço Italia
Bars & clubs
7 Royal Club
Historic buildings walk

Praça da República

In Praça da República the trees are tall and shady. There are also lots of police. Near the Praça is the city's tallest building, the **Edifício Itália** ⓘ *Av Ipiranga 344, T2189 2929, US$8*. There is a restaurant on top and a sightseeing balcony. If you walk up Avenida São Luís, which has many airline offices and travel agencies (especially in Galeria Metrópole), you arrive at Praça Dom José Gaspar, with the **Biblioteca Municipal Mário de Andrade**, surrounded by a pleasant shady garden.

North of the centre

About 10 minutes' walk from the centre is the old **Mercado Municipal** ⓘ *R Cantareira 306, www.mercadomunicipal.com.br, Mon-Sat 0600-1800, Sun 0700-1600*, covering 27,000 sq m. **Parque da Luz** on Avenida Tiradentes (110,000 sq m) was formerly a botanical garden. It is next to the Luz railway station. There are two museums: in the park is the **Pinacoteca do Estado** (State Art Collection) ⓘ *Praça da Luz 2, T3224 1000, www.pinacoteca.org.br, Tue-Sun 1000- 1800, US$3, free on Sat (closes 1730)*. It and its neighbouring sister gallery, the **Estação Pinacoteca** ⓘ *Largo General Osório 66, T3337 0185, daily 1000-1730, US$2, Sat free,* preserve the best collection of modernist Brazilian art outside the Belas Artes in Rio, together with important works by Europeans like Picasso and Chagall. Both have good cafés, the Pinacoteca has a very good art bookshop. Nearby, the **Museu de Arte Sacra** ① *Av Tiradentes 676, T3326 1373, www.museu artesacra.org.br, Tue-Sun 1100-1900, US$2.25*, is modern and tasteful, housed in the serene Igreja e Convento Nossa Senhora da Luz (1774), still partially occupied. It has a priceless, beautifully presented collection including works by Aleijadinho, Benedito Calixto, Mestre Athayde and Francisco Xavier de Brito. The convent is one of the few colonial buildings left in São Paulo; the chapel dates from 1579.

Liberdade

Directly south of the Praça da Sé, and one stop on the Metrô, is Liberdade, the central Japanese district, now also home to large numbers of Koreans and Chinese. The Metrô station is in Praça da Liberdade, in which there is an oriental market every Sunday (see Shopping). The Praça is one of the best places in the city for Japanese food. **Museu da Imigração Japonesa** ① *R São Joaquim 381, exhibition on 7th, 8th and 9th floors, T3209 5465, www.nihonsite.com.br/muse, Tue-Sun 1330-1730, US$2.50*, is excellent, with a roof garden; captions have English summaries.

West of the Old Centre

Jardins and Avenida Paulista → *See map, page 33.*

Avenida Paulista has been transformed since the 1890s from the city's most fashionable promenade into six lanes of traffic lined with banks' and multinationals' headquarters. Its highlight is undoubtedly **MASP**, the common name for the **Museu de Arte de São Paulo** ① *Av Paulista 1578 (above the 9 de Julho tunnel); T3251 5644, www.masp.art.br, Metrô Trianon-MASP; open 1100-1800, except Thu 1100-2000, closed Mon, US$8.20, Tue free*. The museum has the finest collection of European masters in the southern hemisphere with works by artists like Raphael, Bellini, Bosch, Rembrandt, Turner, Constable, Monet, Manet and Renoir. Also some interesting work by Brazilian artists, including Portinari. Temporary exhibitions are also held and when a popular show is on, it can take up to an hour to get in. There is a very good art shop.

Opposite MASP is **Parque Tenente Siqueira Campos** ① *daily 0700-1830*, which covers two blocks on either side of Alameda Santos; a bridge links the two parts of the park. It is block of subtropical forest in the busiest part of the city. In the foyers of some of the nearby towers are various cultural centres (eg **FIESP**, Av Paulista 1313) which put on worthwhile exhibitions and are more-or-less the only sights in the city open on a Monday. The **Museu da Imagem e do Som (MIS)** ① *Av Europa 158, T3085 1498, www.mis.sp.gov.br, Tue-Sun 1000-1800*, has photographic exhibitions, archives of Brazilian cinema and music, and a nice café. Next to MIS is the **Museu Brasiliero da Escultura** (MuBE); free to temporary exhibitions and recitals in the afternoons. Avenida Europa continues to Avenida Brigadeiro Faria Lima, on which is the **Casa Brasileira** ① *Av Faria Lima 2705, T3032 3727, www.mcb.sp.gov.br, Tue-Sun 1000-1800, US$2.20*, a museum of Brazilian furniture. It also holds temporary exhibitions.

Cidade Universitária and Morumbi

The Cidade Universitária is on the west bank of the Rio Pinheiros, opposite the district of Pinheiros. The campus also contains the famous **Instituto Butantan** (Butantan Snake Farm and Museum) ① *Av Dr Vital Brasil 1500, T011-3726 7222, Tue-Sun 0845-1615, www.butantan.gov.br, US$5, children half price under 12, under 7 free, Metrô Butantan.* The

③ Jardins & Avenida Paulista

São Paulo maps
1 São Paulo, page 28
2 São Paulo centre, page 30
3 Jardins & Avenida Paulista, page 33

500 metres (approx)
500 yards (approx)

Where to stay ⬛
1 Dona Zilah *A2*
2 Emiliano *B2*
3 Fasano *B2*
4 Ibis São Paulo Paulista *A3*
5 Landmark Residence *B2*
6 Paulista Garden *C2*
7 Pousada dos Franceses *C3*
8 Renaissance *B3*
9 Transamérica Ópera *B2*
10 Unique *C2*
11 Vila Madalena Hostel *A1*

Restaurants 🍴
1 A Mineira *C3*
2 Baalbeck *B2*
3 Charlô Bistro & Dalva e Dito *B2*
4 Cheiro Verde *B2*
5 DOM *B2*
6 Dui *A2*
7 Figueira Rubaiyat *B1*
8 Fran's Café *B2/C3*
9 Gero *B2*
10 Jun Sakamoto *A1*
11 Kayomix *A2*
12 La Tambouille *C1*
13 Mani *B1*
14 MASP *B3*
15 Massimo *B3*
16 Sattva *A2*
17 Sujinho *A3*
18 Vento Haragano *A2*

Bars & clubs 🍸
19 Bar Balcão *A2*
20 Casa de Francisca *C3*
21 Finnegan's Pub *A1*
22 Outs Club *A3*
23 Sonique *A3*
24 Studio SP *A3*
25 Volt *A3*

instituto's collection of preserved snakes, spiders and scorpions was destroyed by fire in May 2010. The museum and vivarium are open to visitors. The **Museu de Arte Contemporâneo** (**MAC**) ⓘ *T3091 3538, www.mac.usp.br, Tue-Sun 1000-1900, free*, with an important collection of Brazilian and European modern art, is in the Prédio Novo da Reitoria. Also the **Museu de Arqueologia e Etnologia** (MAE) ⓘ *R Reitoria 1466, T3091 4905*, with Amazonian and ancient Mediterranean collections. Not far from the Butantã Institute, just inside Cidade Universitária, is the **Casa do Bandeirante** ⓘ *Praça Monteiro Lobato, T3031 0920, Tue-Sun 0900-1700*, the reconstructed home of a 17th-century pioneer.

On the west bank of the Rio Pinheiros, just southeast of the Cidade Universitária, is the palatial **Jóquei Clube/Jockey Club** ⓘ *Av Lineu de Paula Machado 1263, T2161 8300, www.jockeysp.com.br*, racecourse in the Cidade Jardim area. Take Butantã bus from República. Race meetings are held Monday and Thursday at 1930 and weekends at 1430. It has a **Museu do Turfe** ⓘ *Tue-Sun, closed Sat-Sun mornings*.

Morumbi is a smart residential district due south of the Cidade Universitária. In the area are the state government building, **Palácio dos Bandeirantes** ⓘ *Av Morumbi 4500*, the small, simple **Capela de Morumbi** ⓘ *Av Morumbi 5387*, and the Morumbi stadium of São Paulo Football Club, which holds 100,000 people. Motor racing fans might like to visit the Morumbi cemetery, last resting place of Ayrton Senna; take 6291 bus to Rua Profesor Benedito Montenegro.

Museu da Fundação Maria Luisa e Oscar Americano ⓘ *Av Morumbi 4077, Morumbi, T3742 0077, www.fundacaooscaramericano.org.br, Tue-Sun 1000-1730, US$4*, is a private collection of Brazilian and Portuguese art and furniture. The garden has fascinating paths, patios and plants; concerts are held on Sunday and courses through the week. It is close to the Palácio dos Bandeirantes.

Burle Marx Park ⓘ *Av Dona Helena Pereira de Moraes 200, Morumbi, daily 0700-1900*. Designed by famous landscape designer Burle Marx, it has trails leading through the Mata Atlântica (Atlantic rainforest).

South of the Old Centre

Ibirapuera

The **Parque do Ibirapuera** ⓘ *entrance on Av Pedro Álvares Cabral, daily 0600-1730*, was designed by Oscar Niemeyer and landscape artist Roberto Burle Marx for the city's fourth centenary in 1954. Within its 160 ha is the **Assembléia Legislativa** and a **planetarium** ⓘ *T5575 5206, Sat, Sun 1200-1800, US$5*. After many years of refurbishment it now has state-of-the-art fittings. Buy tickets 30 minutes before the show. Also in the park is the **Museu de Arte Moderna** (MAM) ⓘ *T5085 1300, www.mam.org.br, Tue-Sun 1000-1800, US$2.75*, with art exhibitions and sculpture garden (see Nuno Ramos' Craca – Barnacle). It has a great café restaurant and art shop. **Museu Afro-Brasileiro** ⓘ *T5579 0593, Wed-Sun 1000-1800, free*: temporary exhibitions, theatre, dance and cinema spaces, photographs and panels devoted to exploring African Brazil. **Pavilhão Japonês** ⓘ *T3573 6543, Sat, Sun 1000-1700, free except for exhibitions*, exhibition space showing works from Japanese and Japanese-Brazilian artists, designed by Japanese and built exclusively with materials from Japan. It is set in Japanese gardens and has a traditional tea house upstairs. Bicycles can be hired in the park, US$3 per hour. Buses to Ibirapuera, 574R from Paraíso Metrô station; 6364 from Praça da Bandeira; to Cidade Universitária 702U or 7181 from Praça da República. Every even-numbered year the

Bienal Internacional de São Paulo (São Paulo Biennial) at Ibirapuera has the most important show of modern art in Latin America, usually in September (next in 2012).

Parque da Independência
In the suburb of Ipiranga, 5.5 km southeast of the city centre, the Parque da Independência contains the **Monumento à Independência**. Beneath the monument is the Imperial Chapel ① *Tue-Sun 1300-1700*, with the tomb of the first emperor, Dom Pedro I, and Empress Leopoldina. **Casa do Grito** ① *Tue-Sun 0930-1700*, the little house in which Dom Pedro I spent the night before his famous cry of Ipiranga, 'Independence or Death', is preserved in the park. The **Museu Paulista** ① *T6165 8000, Tue-Sun 0900-1645, US$1*, contains old maps, traditional furniture, collections of old coins, religious art and *indígena* ethnology. Behind the Museum is the **Horto Botânico (Ipiranga Botanical Garden)** and the **Jardim Francês** ① *Tue-Sun 0900-1700, getting there: take bus 478-P (Ipiranga-Pompéia for return) from Ana Rosa, or take bus 4612 from Praça da República.*

Parque do Estado (Jardim Botânico)
This large park, a long way south of the centre, at **Água Funda** ① *Av Miguel Estefano 3031-3687, T5573 6300, Wed-Sun 0900-1700, getting there: take Metrô to São Judas on the Jabaquara line, then take a bus*, contains the Jardim Botânico, with lakes and trees and places for picnics, and a very fine orchid farm worth seeing during November-December (orchid exhibitions in April and November).

❂ São Paulo listings

For hotel and restaurant price codes and other relevant information, see pages 9-12.

🛏 Where to stay

For both business and leisure, São Paulo has by far the best hotels in Brazil. The best area to stay is northeastern Jardins (also known as Cerqueria César), which is safe and well connected to the Metrô via Av Paulista. There are cheapies in the centre, but this is an undesirable area at night.

Jardins, Avenida Paulista and around
p32, map p33

$$$$ Emiliano, R Oscar Freire 384, T3069 4369, www.emiliano.com.br. Bright and beautifully designed, attention to every detail and the best suites in the city. No pool but a relaxing small spa. Excellent Italian restaurant, location and service.

$$$$ Fasano, R Vittorio Fasano 88, T3896 4077, www.fasano.com.br. One of the world's great hotels with decor like a modernist gentleman's club designed by Armani, a fabulous pool and the best formal haute cuisine restaurant in Brazil. Excellently positioned in Jardins.

$$$$ Unique, Av Brigadeiro Luis Antônio 4700, Jardim Paulista, T3055 4700, www.hotel unique.com. The most ostentatious hotel in the country, an enormous half moon on concrete uprights with curving floors, circular windows and beautiful use of space and light. The bar on the top floor is São Paulo's answer to the LA Sky Bar and is always filled with the rich and famous after 2130.

$$$ Dona Zíláh, Al França 1621, Jardim Paulista, T3062 1444, www.zilah.com. Little pousada in a renovated colonial house, well maintained, decorated with a personal touch. Excellent location, bike rental and generous breakfast included.

$$$ Formule 1 Paraíso, R Vergueiro 1571, T5085 5699, www.accorhotels.com.br.

Another great value business-style hotel, apartments big enough for 3 make this an economic option for those in a group. Right next to Paraíso Metro in a safe area, a/c.

$$$ Ibis São Paulo Paulista, Av Paulista 2355, T3523 3000, www.accorhotels.com.br. Great value, modern business standard rooms with a/c, right on Paulista, cheaper Sat-Sun.

$$$ Paulista Garden, Al Lorena 21, T/F3885 8498, www.paulistagardenhotel.com.br. Small, simple rooms with a/c, cable TV and fridge, close to Ibirapuera Park.

$$$-$$ Pousada dos Franceses, R dos Franceses 100, Bela Vista, T3288 1592, www.pousadados franceses.com.br. Plain little pousada 10 mins' walk from Brigadeiro Metrô. dorms, doubles and singles, free internet, TV room, breakfast included.

$$$-$ Vila Madalena Hostel, R Francisco Leitão 686, T3034 4104, www.vilamadalenahostel.com. Price for double bed US$24-30 in dorms for 4 or 8. 15 mins from Clínicas Metrô, well-run, popular, arty hostel with good services, bikes for rent, internet and Wi-Fi.

$$-$ Casa Club, R Mourata Coelho 973, Vila Madalena, T3798 0051, www.casaclub.com.br. Tiny hostel with shared rooms that can be booked privately, one for women only. Previously a bar and retains its party atmosphere, Wi-Fi, restaurant.

$$-$ Sampa Hostel, R Girassol 519, Vila Madalena, T3031 6779, www.sampa hostel.com.br. Dorms (US$20-25) and 2 private rooms which need booking in advance, convenient, with fan, breakfast, Wi-Fi.

⊘ Restaurants

Jardins p32, map p33

Those on a budget can eat to their stomach's content in per kg places or, cheaper still, bakeries (padarias) There's one on almost every corner and they serve sandwiches, delicious Brazilian burgers made from decent meat and served with ham, egg, cheese or salad. They always have good coffee, juices, cakes and set lunches (almoços) for a very economical price. Most have a designated sitting area – either at the padaria bar or in an adjacent room. Juices are made from mineral or filtered water.

$$$ Charlô Bistro, R Barão de Capanema 440 (next to DOM), T3088 6790 (with another branch at the Jockey Club, Av Lineu de Paula Machado 1263, Cidade Jardim, T3034 3682). One of the premier VIP and old family haunts in the city run by a scion of one of the city's establishment families. Decked out in tribute to a Paris brasserie and with food to match.

$$$ DOM, R Barão de Capanema 549, T3088 0761. Jardins' evening restaurant of the moment – Alex Attala has won the coveted Veja best chef of the year award twice. Contemporary food, fusing Brazilian ingredients with French and Italian styles and served in a large modernist dining room.

$$$ Fasano, in Hotel Fasano (see Where to stay), T3896 4077. Long regarded as the leading gourmet restaurant in São Paulo. A huge choice of modern Italian and French cooking from chef Salvatore Loi. Diners have their own lowly lit booths in a magnificent dining room, exemplary wine list, formal dress.

$$$ Figueira Rubaiyat, R Haddock Lobo 1738, T3063 3888. The most interesting of the Rubaiyat restaurant group, supervised by Argentinian chef Francis Mallman. Very lively for Sun lunch, light and airy and under a huge tropical fig tree. The best meat is served at another restaurant in the chain, **Baby Beef Rubaiyat**, Av Brig Faria Lima 2954, T3078 9488.

$$$ Gero, R Haddock Lobo 1629, T3064 0005. Fasano's version of a French Bistrô a Côté, but serving pasta and light Italian. Ever so casual design; be prepared for a long wait at the bar alongside people who are there principally to be seen. Reservations are not accepted.

$$$ Jun Sakamoto, R Lisboa 55, T3088 6019. Japanese with a touch of French; superb fresh ingredients (some of it flown in especially from Asia and the USA).

$$$ La Tambouille, Av 9 de Julho 5925, Jardim Europa, T3079 6276. The favourite 'old money' Franco-Italian restaurant. Excellent wine list.

$$$ Massimo, Al Santos 1826, Cerqueira César, T3284 0311. One of São Paulo's longest established Italian restaurants serving Northern Italian food. Credit cards are not accepted, despite the costly price.

$$$ Vento Haragano, Av Rebouças 1001, T3083 4265. One of the best rodízios in the city.

$$ A Mineira, Al Joaquim Eugénio de Lima 697, T3283 2349. Self-service Minas food by the kilo. Lots of choice., with Cachaça and pudding included.

$$ Baalbeck, Al Lorena 1330, T3088 4820. Lebanese cooking vastly superior to its luncheonette setting. Great falafel.

$$ Fran's Café, Av Paulista 358, and throughout the city. Open 24 hrs, the Brazilian equivalent of Starbuck's but with proper coffee and light meals.

$$ Kayomix, R da Consolação 3215, T3082 2769. Brazilian Oriental fusions like salmon taratare with shimeji and shitake.

$$RR **Restaurante do MASP**, Av Paulista 1578, T3253 2829. In the basement of the museum, reasonably priced standards like lasagna and stroganoff often with a garnish of live music.

$$ Sujinho, R da Consolação 2068, Consolação, T3256 8026. South American beef in large portions, other carnivorous options also available.

$ Cheiro Verde, R Peixoto Gomide 1413, T289 6853 (lunch only). Hearty veggie food, like vegetable crumble in gorgonzola sauce and pasta with buffalo mozarella and sun-dried tomato.

🍸 Bars and clubs

The best places for nightlife are Itaim, Moema and Vila Olímpia, and Vila Madalena/Pinheiros. Jardins' best bars are in the top hotels. Vila Olímpia, Itaim and Moema have a series of funky, smart bars overflowing onto

the street, filled with an eclectic mix of after-workers, clubbers, singles and couples; all united by being under 40 and having money. These sit alongside imitation US and European club/lounge bars playing techno, hip hop and the like. The busiest streets for a bar wander are Rua Atílio Inocenti near the junction of Av Juscelino Kubitschek and Av Brigadeiro Faria Lima, Av Hélio Pellegrino and Rua Araguari, which runs behind it. Vila Madalena is younger still, more hippy-chic, but is the best part of town to hear live, Brazilian music and uniquely Brazilian close dances like Forró, as opposed to international club sounds. The liveliest streets are Aspicuelta and Girassol.

Jardins *p32, map p33*

Bar Balcão, R Dr Melo Alves 150, T3063 6091. After work meeting place, very popular with young professionals and media types who gather on either side of the long low wooden bar which winds its way around the room like a giant snake.

Finnegan's Pub, R Cristiano Viana 358, Pinheiros. One of São Paulo's various Irish bars, this one actually run by an Irishman, popular with ex-pats.

🚍 Transport

São Paulo *p26, maps p28, p30 and p33*
Air From the international airport **Guarulhos** (also known as Cumbica), T6445 2945, there are airport taxis which charge US$65 on a ticket system (the taxi offices are outside Customs, 300 m down on the left; go to get your ticket then take your bags right back to the end of the taxi queue). Fares from the city to the airport are slightly less and vary from cab to cab. Various **Emtubus** city buses (www.emtu.sp.gov.br) run from Guarulhos to Praça da República, Congonhas airport, Barra Funda terminal, Itaim Bibi and a circuit of hotels, US$19; also to Tatuapé Metrô station, US$2.50. **Pássaro Marron** airport bus service, T0800-770 7995, Mon-Fri 0700-1900,

weekends T2445-2430, www.airport buservice.com.br, also run buses between Guarulhos, the city centre, rodoviárias, Congonhas airport, Avenida Paulista and Jardins hotels, etc; frequent service 0500-2330 (0430 to Tietê), US$12.50. From **Congonhas airport**, there are about 400 flights a week to Rio. Taxi Congonhas airport-Jardins is US$19.

Airport information Money exchanges, in the arrivals hall, Guarulhos, 0800-2200 daily. Post office on the 3rd floor of Asa A. See page 26, for the tourist office.

Bus City buses are run by **SP Trans**, www.sptrans.com.br. You can work out your route on the planner on the bus company's website and on Google maps, which mark bus stops. These maps, plus those on the Metrô and **CPTM** websites (see below) will give you a good coverage of the city. Even if you do not speak Portuguese they are fairly self-explanatory. Local transport maps are also available at stations and depots. Some city bus routes are run by trolley buses. City bus fare is US$1.65.

Metrô The best and cheapest way to get around São Paulo is on the excellent metrô system, daily 0500-2400, www.metro.sp.gov.br, with a clear journey planner and information in Portuguese and English. It is clean, safe, cheap and efficient and has 5 main lines. It is integrated with the overground **CPTM**

(Companhia Paulista de Trens Metropolitanos), www.cptm.sp.gov.br, an urban light railway which serves to extend the metrô along the margins of the Tietê and Pinheiros rivers and to the outer city suburbs. There are 6 lines, numbers 7 to 12, which are colour-coded like the metrô. Information T0800-055 0121. Fare US$1.65; backpacks are allowed. Combined bus and Metrô ticket are available, US$2.55. The *bilhete único* integrates bus, metro and light railway in a single, rechargeable plastic swipe card. US$2.55 serves for 1 metro or CPTM journey and 3 bus journeys within the space of 3 hrs (1 unit). Swipe cards can be bought at metro stations. The initial minimum charge is equivalent to 5 units. Swipe cards can be bought at thousands of authorised outlets, including SP Trans' own shops (eg Praça da Sé 188, R Augusta 449), metro stations, newsstands, lottery shops, etc.

Taxi Taxis display cards of actual tariffs in the window (starting price US$4). There are ordinary taxis, which are hailed on the street, or at taxi stations such as Praça da República, radio taxis and deluxe taxis. For **Radio Taxis**, which are more expensive but involve fewer hassles, **Central Radio Táxi**, T3035 0404, www.centralradiotaxi.com; **São Paulo Rádio Táxi**, T5073 2814. Visit www.taxisp.com.br for a list or look in the phone book; calls are not accepted from public phones.

Contents

Border crossings

Brazil–Bolivia
Corumbá–Puerto Suárez, page 55
Cáceres–San Matías, page 69

Brazil–Paraguay
Ponta Porã–Pedro Juan Caballero,
  page 48

The Pantanal

The Pantanal UNESCO Biosphere Reserve is the world's largest freshwater wetland and one of the best places on earth for seeing wildlife, particularly birds. Within Brazil it comprises a plain of around 21,000 sq km but the Pantanal extends beyond Brazil into Bolivia, Paraguay and Argentina to form an area totalling 100,000 sq km. The plain slopes 1 cm in every kilometre north to south and west to east to the basin of the Rio Paraguai and is rimmed by low mountains. From these, 175 rivers flow into the Pantanal and after the heavy summer rains they burst their banks, as does the Paraguai itself, to create vast shallow lakes broken by patches of high ground and stands of cerrado forest. Plankton then swarm in the water to form a biological soup that contains as many as 500 million micro algae per litre. Millions of amphibians and fish spawn or migrate to consume them. And these in turn are preyed upon by waterbirds and reptiles. Herbivorous mammals graze on the stands of water hyacinth, sedge and savannah grass and at the top of the food chain lie South America's great predators – the jaguar, ocelot, maned wolf and yellow anaconda. In June, at the end of the wet season, when the sheets of water have reduced, wildlife concentrates around the small lakes or canals and then there is nowhere else on earth that you will see such vast quantities of birds or such enormous numbers of crocodilians. Only the plains of Africa can compete for mammals and your chances of seeing a jaguar or one of Brazil's seven other species of wild cat are greater here than anywhere on the continent.

Background

To the indigenous groups who arrived in the area tens of thousands of years before the Europeans, the Pantanal was a sea, which they called 'Xaraes'. Myths about this sea quickly reached the ears of the Spanish and Portuguese *conquistadores*, who set out to explore it. As if to presage the future, the first to arrive, in 1543, was a Spaniard called Cabeza de Vaca (Cow Head) who complained about the swarms of mosquitoes and vampire bats and promptly turned westward into the Paraguayan *chaco*. The fate of the Pantanal and its myriad indigenous residents was left to the ruthless Portuguese and their *bandeirantes*. Apart from a few skirmishes they left the Pantanal alone for 200 years, but then gold was discovered glittering in a stream they called the River of Stars (or 'Cuiabá' by the local people). A settlement was established and soon the Portuguese were scouring the area for native slave labour for their mines. The *indígenas* were understandably aggrieved by this and two of the fiercest tribes, the Guaicurú and the Paiaguá, combined forces to attack the Portuguese. Their tactics were highly effective: they worked in small guerrilla bands, laying ambushes when the Europeans least expected it. The Guiacurú were horsemen, charging into battle naked but for jaguar skins, clubs, lances and machetes; crouched low on their stolen Andalusian horses, or riding on the horse's sides rather than their backs and thus invisible to the Portuguese. They used no saddles or stirrups and had just two chords for reins. The Paiaguá attacked by water and were excellent swimmers, advancing in their canoes and then leaping into the water and using the sides of the boats as shields. They would then suddenly right their boats and fire several volleys of arrows during the time it took the *bandeirantes* to fire one. They soon defeated the Europeans, regaining control of the Pantanal for almost 100 years. The Portuguese were furious and accused the Guaicurú in particular of dishonourable tactics. "They fight only to win," the Portuguese claimed, "attacking only when the enemy seemed weaker". The Guiacurú responded by exposing the hypocrisy of the Portuguese: "Since the Portuguese and Spaniards claim to go to heaven when they die, they do well to die quickly. But, since they also claim that the Guiacurú go to hell after death, in that case the Guiacurú want to die as late as possible." (John Hemming, *Red Gold*). But through subterfuge the pact was broken and in 1734 the Portuguese regained control by means of a devastating ambush that decimated the Paiaguá. The tribes then retreated into the depths of the Pantanal where their numbers slowly diminished as a result of punitive *bandeirantes* expeditions, inter-tribal conflict and European diseases.

Today Pantaneiros boast of their proud traditions, which are barely three generations old. Nearly 25 million of their cattle roam the Pantanal and the true indigenous Pantaneiros have largely disappeared. Of the 25,000 Guiacurú present in 1500, some 200 survive in their Kadiweu and Mbayá subgroups. The Paiaguá have been reduced to a sad remnant living on an island reservation near Asunción in Paraguay. Other tribes, such as the Parecis, who were enslaved in the mines, fared even worse and, of the great indigenous groups of the Pantanal, only the Bororo, who allied with the Portuguese, retain any significant numbers. Even their traditions have been greatly damaged by the aggressive missionary tactics of the Salesians in the 20th century.

Wildlife and vegetation

Wildlife → *See alsoEcology, conservation and environmental concerns, page 44.*

Mammals Outside Africa there is nowhere better for seeing wild mammals than the Pantanal, especially between July and late September. During this time, there are groups of **capybara** – the world's largest rodent – at just about every turn. Critically endangered **marsh deer** (who have webbed feet to help them run through the swamp), or their more timid cousins, the **red brocket**, and the **pampas deer** wander in every other stretch of savannah alongside **giant anteaters**. Few visitors leave without having seen both species of peccary (which resemble pigs but are in a different family) – the solitary **collared peccary** and the herd-living **white-lipped peccary**, **giant otters** and at least one species of cat. Lucky visitors may even see a jaguar or **tapir**. There are at least 102 mammal species here and, although most of them are bats (including vampires), the list includes eight of South America's 10 wild cats, four dog species and numerous primates ranging from the tiny palm-sized **pygmy marmoset** to South America's second largest primate, the **red howler monkey**.

The cats are usually top of everyone's 'most wanted' list. The largest is the **jaguar** (most easily seen here at **Fazenda San Francisco** in the south, or at **Porto Jofre** on the Transpantaneira), followed by the more elusive **puma**, which has the widest distribution of any feline in the world. Even more common is the retriever-sized **ocelot** and the tawny or black **jaguarundi**, twice the size of a domestic cat, though more slender. The most elusive creature is the **pampas cat**, with a fawn body and striped legs, but scientists are yet to agree on its species. The other cats are all spotted and are, in size order, the **margay**, **geoffroy's cat** (the most hunted in the Americas) and, the most beautiful of all, the **oncilla** or tiger cat.

Other carnivores include **crab-eating foxes**, **coatis** and **racoons** (who often hang around the *fazendas* at night), the **maned wolf**, **short-eared dog**, and **bush dog** (Cachorro Vinagre, found in the drier semi-deciduous forests). Monkeys are not as varied here as they are in the Amazon, but visitors will hear or see **red howler monkey** or **black howler monkey**, the smaller **brown capuchin**, and possibly the **pygmy marmoset** or the **silvery marmoset**. Other species present include various **titi monkeys** and **night monkeys**, which are most easily seen around **Fazenda Bela Vista** on the Estrada Parque in the south. Woolly monkeys can be found in the dry forests.

Reptiles After birds, the easiest animals to see in the Pantanal are caimans, of which the dominant species is the **jacaré caiman**, a smaller sub-species of the spectacled caiman found in the Amazon. Jacaré caimans reach a maximum length of about 1.5 m. **Yellow anaconda**, the world's heaviest snake, are abundant but difficult to see; your best chance is on the Estrada Parque in the south, which they frequently cross during the day. Other snakes, the majority of which are not venomous, are also abundant but hard to spot. The venomous species, which include pit vipers, such as the **fer de lance** or jararaca, are nocturnal.

Birds There are more than 700 resident and migratory bird species in the Pantanal. Birding on the Transpantaneira road in the north or at one of the *fazendas* in the south can yield as many as 100 species a day. From late June to early October there are vast numbers of birds. Try to visit as many habitat types as possible and, as well as trail-walking, jeep rides and horse riding, include river trips in your itinerary. Night safaris will maximize sightings of more unusual **heron**, such as the boat-billed, agami and zigzag, and the numerous nightjars and potoos. Specialities in the Pantanal include the 1-m-long **hyacinth macaw** (the world's largest parrot), the **golden-collared macaw, blue-fronted parrot, blue-crowned nanday, blaze-winged and green-cheeked parakeets**, the giant flightless **rhea**, chestnut-bellied and spix's **guan, crowned eagle, bare faced currasow** and **helmeted manakin**. Bring good binoculars and a field guide. Nigel Wheatley's *Where to watch birds in South America* can give far greater detail than this book has space for, though it is now very out of date.

Forest types and what lives where

Although the Pantanal is often described as an ecosystem in its own right, it is actually made up of many habitats, which have their own, often distinct, biological communities. The Pantanal is of recent geological origin and has very few endemic plant species. Botanically it is a mosaic: a mixture of elements from the Amazon region including *varzea* and gallery forests and tropical savannah, the *cerrado* of central Brazil and the dry *chaco* region of Paraguay.

Pantanal cerrado forest The *cerrado* is found both in the upland areas, which are not prone to flooding, and in some areas that may be inundated for a short period. It is dominated by the *cerrado* **pequi tree** (*Caryocar brasiliense*) whose fruits have a famous spiny interior, the beautiful flowering legume **Sucupira** (*Bowdichia virgiloides*) and the **sandpaper tree** (*Curatella americana*). But the most conspicuous trees in the *cerrado* are **trumpet trees** (various *ipê*); these are characterized by their brilliant colours (indigo in *Tabebuia impetignosa* and yellow in *Tabebuia aurea*) and no leaves in the dry season. Sometimes these trees stand as the dominant species in vast areas of semi-agrarian parkland. Within the dry *cerrado* are numerous stands of **bocaiúva palm** (*Acrocomia aculeate*) characterized by its very spiny trunk and leaves. Its fruit is an important food source for macaws and larger parrots. In the wetter *cerrado* are numerous islands of dense savannah forest or *cerradão*, often thick with **acuri palm** (*Attalea phalerata*), whose woody fruit is the principal food for the hyacinth macaw and, when fallen, for peccaries (*javali* in Portuguese) and agouti (rabbit-sized, tailless rodents; *cutia* in Portuguese). *Cerrado* habitats are also important refuges for the larger sheltering mammals, such as jaguar and tapir, who will flee into the densest wet *cerrado* to escape predators.

Semi-deciduous tropical forest This taller, denser forest occurs on higher ground such as the Serra do Bodoquena south of Miranda, and comprises a mix of species from the Paraguayan *chaco* and the Amazon. For instance **jutai** (*Hymenaea courbaril*), from which the sacred copal resin is extracted, comes from the Amazon; while the **monkey-ear plant** (*Enterolobium contortisquam*), recognized by its curved seed pods, is a common *chaco* species. More primate species can be found here than elsewhere in the Pantanal, along with smaller toucans, such as the **chestnut eared aracari**, and rare mammals like bush dog and **tayra** (*Iara*).

Swamp and seasonally flooded land This varies greatly, from Amazonian habitats characterized by riverine forests such as *varzea* (seasonally flooded riverbank forest) to seasonally flooded grassland and palm savannah dominated by **carunda palm** trees. Alongside these are permanently marshy areas and open lakes and oxbows thick with floating plants. This diversity of habitats means a great diversity of species and nowhere is better than these areas for seeing large concentrations of birds and mammals. *Varzea*, which is best seen by canoe or paddle boat, is good for mammals such as tapir and giant otter, and for riverine birds like the **southern screamer** (*tachá*), the five species of Brazilian **kingfisher** (*Martim pescador*), **black-collared hawks** (*Gaviao belo*) and many species of heron and stork, including the giant 1.2-m-tall **jabiru** (*tuiuiu*). Apart from *varzea*, much swampland is dominated by the papyrus-like sedge (*Cyperus giganteus*) or reed mace (*Typha dominguensis*) or by floating plants like **water hyacinth** (*Eichhornia crassipes*), which caiman and capybara use as cover.

Xeric vegetation This permanently dry scrub forest found in elevated areas is dominated by *chaco* species such as various types of **cacti** (such as *Cereus peruvianus* and *Opuntia stenarthra*) together with the swollen-trunked, baobab-like pot-bellied **chorisia** (*Bombacaceae*). Many distinct species occur here, including one of the world's rarest cats, the pampas cat, and rare birds, such as **black-legged seriemas** and *chaco* **earthcreepers**.

Ecology, conservation and environmental concerns

Only one area of the Pantanal is officially a national park, the 135,000-ha **Parque Nacional do Pantanal Matogrossense** in the municipality of Poconé, only accessible by air or river. Obtain permission to visit from **Instituto Chico Mendes de Conservação da Biodiversidade (ICMBio)**, www.icmbio.gov.br. Hunting is strictly forbidden throughout the Pantanal and is punishable by four years' imprisonment. However, most *fazendeiros* regularly shoot and kill jaguar, many locals are still jaguar hunters and some landowners even allow illegal private hunts.

Fishing is allowed with a licence, US$40, according to strict quotas. It is not permitted in the spawning season or *piracema* (1 October to 1 February in Mato Grosso do Sul; 1 November to 1 March in Mato Grosso). There are also restrictions on the size of fish that may be caught, but poaching is rife and there are plans to halt all fishing for a few years due to severe stock depletion. Application forms are available through travel agents with advance notice. Catch and release is the only kind of fishing allowed on rivers Abobral, Negro, Perdido and Vermelho. Like other wilderness areas, the Pantanal faces significant threats. Agrochemicals and *garimpo* mercury, washed down from the neighbouring *planalto*, are a hazard.

The **International Union for the Conservation of Nature** (IUCN), www.iucn.org, is concerned at the amount of poaching, particularly of *jacaré* skins, birds and capybara. The forestry police have built control points on all major access roads to the Pantanal. Biologists interested in research projects should contact the **Coordenador de Estudos do Pantanal** ① *Departamento de Biologia, Universidade Federal do Mato Grosso do Sul, Campo Grande, T067-3787 3311 ext 2113*, or **Projeto Gadonça** ① *Fazenda San Francisco, www.fazenda sanfrancisco.tur.br*. See also **Fazenda San Francisco**, page 58.

There have been serious concerns about the **Southwild Jaguar Camp**, on the Transpantaneira, who stands accused, by the Ministério Público de Mato Grosso, of feeding wild jaguar to lure them to the camera, building on national park land and of attempted animal trafficking. We do not recommend them nor any who guarantee a jaguar sighting.

Visitors can make an important contribution to protecting the Pantanal by acting responsibly and choosing guides accordingly. Take your rubbish away with you, don't fish out of season, don't let guides kill or disturb fauna, don't buy products made from endangered species, don't buy live birds or monkeys, and report any violation to the authorities. The practice of catching caiman, even though they are then released, is traumatic for the animals and has potentially disruptive long-term effects.

Mato Grosso do Sul and the Southern Pantanal

Mato Grosso do Sul is dominated by the Pantanal wetlands in the north and by the low Serra da Bodoquena mountains in the south, which surround the family-orientated ecotourism town of Bonito. The mountains are honeycombed by caves and cut by numerous glassy clear streams. There are only a few towns of any size and the state is a centre of soya plantations and cattle ranching. Many of the designated backpacker tours of the Pantanal leave from the state capital, Campo Grande, which is a prosperous, modern city with lively nightlife. However, they take half a day to reach the Pantanal itself, which begins in earnest east of Campo Grande, near the cattle-ranching town of Miranda. Many of the best fazenda ranch houses are in the area surrounding Miranda, as well as a handful of small, upmarket tour operators. The town also has one of the Pantanal's liveliest festivals, O Festa do Homen Pantaneiro, in November. Corumbá, on the banks of the Rio Paraguai, is another popular departure point for the Pantanal, and lies close to the Estrada Parque dirt road (which runs through the wetlands) and to Nhecolândia, a wilderness area visited by most of the Campo Grande backpacker tours. ⇥ *For listings, see pages 56-64.*

Campo Grande → *For listings, see pages 56-64. Phone code: 067. Population: 665,000.*

A major gateway to the Pantanal, Campo Grande is a pleasant, modern city on a grid system, with wide avenues. It was founded in 1899 and became the state capital in 1979. Because of the *terra roxa* (red earth), it is known as the 'Cidade Morena'.

In the centre is a shady park, the **Praça República**, commonly called the Praça do Rádio after the Rádio Clube on one of its corners. Three blocks west is **Praça Ari Coelho**. Linking the two squares, and running east–west through the city, is the broad Avenida Afonso Pena; much of its central reservation is planted with yellow *ypé* trees. In spring, their blossom covers the avenue, and much of the city besides. The avenue's eastern reaches are the centre of a burgeoning restaurant and nightlife scene. City tours are on offer everywhere but they are generally expensive and there are few obvious sights.

Arriving in Campo Grande

Getting there The **airport** ⓘ *Av Duque de Caxias, 7 km, T067-3368 6000,* receives flights from Cuiabá, Londrina, São Paulo and Santa Cruz (Bolivia). A bus leaves every 10 minutes from outside the airport terminal for the city centre and bus station. A taxi costs US$6 (10 minutes). It is safe to spend the night at the airport if you arrive late. Banco do Brasil at the airport exchanges dollars; the Bradesco just outside has a Visa ATM. The airport also has a tourist information booth (little English, many pamphlets), a post office, car rental and airline offices.

Campo Grande is well connected by bus to cities in the southern Pantanal and onwards to Bolivia and Paraguay, and to São Paulo, Cuiabá and Brasília/Goiânia. The new **rodoviária** is 15km outside the city centre on Av Gury Marques (BR-163) 1215. The terminal has cafes, internet, a handful of shops and left luggage. Most Pantanal tour operators will meet clients off the bus and organise transfers to destinations further afield. Bus 087 leaves every 20 mins from Praça Ari Coelho in the centre, US$1.50, shuttle bus to the airport US$5, taxi to the centre US$17.

The **Trem do Pantanal** train connects Campo Grande with Miranda at weekends – see Miranda, page 51, for more details.

The BR-262 is paved most of the way from Campo Grande to Corumbá and the Bolivian border; a rail service along this route is due to recommence in early 2009 and is likely to be expensive. It is best to make this journey during the day to take advantage of the marvellous scenery. ▸▸ *See Transport, page 62.*

Tourist information There are **Centro de Atendimento ao Turista** ⓘ *www.prefeiturade campogrande.com.br, Mon-Fri 0900-1800,* tourist booths throughout the city: at the airport, T067-3363 3116; in the rodoviária, T067-3382 2350; and in the Mercado Municipal, T067-3314 9949.

Places in Campo Grande

Just north of the Praça República, is the **Museu Dom Bosco** ⓘ *Av Alfonso Pena, Parque Naçoes Indígenas, T067-3312 6491, www.museu.ucdb.br, usually Tue-Sat 0800-1800, Sun 0800-1200 and 1400-1700, US$1.50, but with a temporary restriction on visits in early 2009, contact Professor Dirceu or Señor Juliano on T067-3326 9788,* which contains relics of the tribes who suffered at the hands of aggressive Salesian missionaries in the early and mid-20th century. The largest collections are from the Tukano and Bororo people from the upper Rio Negro and Mato Grosso respectively, both of whose cultures the Salesians were responsible for almost completely wiping out. Traditional practices such as sleeping in *malocas* or wearing indigenous clothing were banned, and the *indígenas* were indoctrinated in rigorous, literalistic pre-Vatican II Catholicism. These exhibits sit alongside a rather depressing display of stuffed endangered species (mostly from the Pantanal), as well as peculiarities such as a two-headed calf, and seashells from around the world.

Next to the railway line, the **Museu do Arte Contemporâneo** ⓘ *Marechal Rondón and Av Calógeras, Mon-Fri 1300-1800, free,* displays modern art from the region.

The **Parque dos Poderes**, a long way from the centre, covers several hectares. As well as the Palácio do Governo and state secretariats, there is a small zoo for rehabilitating animals from the Pantanal. Contact the **Centro de Reabilitação de Animais Silvestres**

(CRAS) ① *T067-3326 1370*, to arrange a visit. There are many lovely trees in the park, along with cycling and jogging tracks. Plenty of capybara live in the lakes.

Coxim → *Phone code: 067. Population: 28,500.*

Coxim, 242 km north of Campo Grande on the BR-163 and halfway between Campo Grande and Rondonópolis, also provides access to the Pantanal. It sits in a green bowl, on the shores of the Rio Taquari. The area has great potential for tourism, with waterfalls nearby at Palmeiras, and the Pantanal in close proximity. But as yet there are no official tours other than a few small charter boat operators at the town port. There are a few hotels including some cheap options around the bus station.

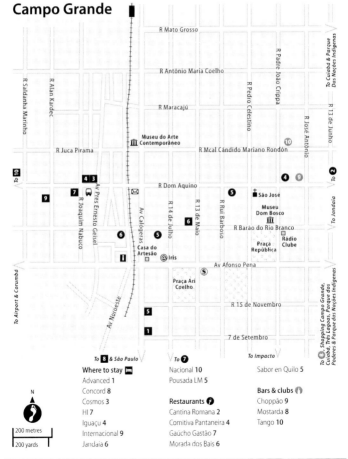

Campo Grande

Where to stay 🛏
Advanced 1
Concord 8
Cosmos 3
HI 7
Iguaçu 4
Internacional 9
Jaraidaia 6

Nacional 10
Pousada LM 5

Restaurants 🍴
Cantina Romana 2
Comitiva Pantaneira 4
Gaúcho Gastão 7
Morada dos Bais 6

Sabor en Quilo 5

Bars & clubs 🍸
Choppão 9
Mostarda 8
Tango 10

Border essentials: Brazil–Paraguay

Ponta Porã (Brazil)–Pedro Juan Caballero (Paraguay)

Immigration There are no border posts between the two towns and people pass freely for local visits. For entry/exit visas, go to the **Brazilian Federal Police office**, Rua Marechal Floriano 1483 (second floor of the white engineering supply company building), T067-3431 1428, Monday to Friday 0730-1130, 1400-1700. The two nations' consulates face each other on Rua Internacional (border street), a block west of Ponta Porã's local bus terminal; some nationalities require a visa from the **Paraguayan consul**, Rua Internacional, next to Hotel Internacional, Monday to Friday 0800-1200. Check requirements carefully, and ensure your documents are in order; without the proper stamps you will inevitably be sent back somewhere later on in your travels. Taking a taxi between offices can speed things up if pressed for time; drivers know about border crossing requirements, US$7.

Transport From the border, there are frequent buses (around six hours) to Asunción, and flights there from Pedro Juan Caballero. A road also runs to Concepción on the Rio Paraguai, where boat connections can be made.

Ponta Porã to the border → *For listings, see pages 56-64. Phone code: 067. Population: 54,000.*

Right on the border, Ponta Porã is separated from the town of **Pedro Juan Caballero** in Paraguay by only a broad avenue. With paved streets, good public transport and smart shops, Ponta Porã is decidedly more prosperous than its neighbour, although Brazilian visitors flock across the border to play the casino and buy cheaper foreign goods. An animal show is held each October at the **Parque das Exposições**, by the *rodoviária*.

The town can be reached by bus or plane from Campo Grande. The *rodoviária* is 3 km out on the Dourados road, from where the 'São Domingos' bus runs to the centre, taxi US$3.

Bonito and around → *For listings, see pages 56-64. See also map, page 50. Phone code: 067. Population: 17,000.*

The designated tourist town of Bonito lies just south of the Pantanal in the **Serra da Bodoquena** hills. It is surrounded by beautiful *cerrado* forest cut by clear-water rivers rich with fish and dotted with plunging waterfalls and deep caves. The town was 'discovered' by *Globo* television in the 1980s and has since grown to become Brazil's foremost ecotourism destination. There are plenty of opportunities for gentle adventure activities such as caving, rafting and snorkelling, all with proper safety measures and great even for very small children. Those looking to see animals and contemplate nature should opt for the forest walks of the Sucuri river. Despite the heavy influx of visitors, plenty of wildlife appear on and around the trails when it is quiet. **Paca** and **agouti** (large, tailless foraging rodents), **brown capuchin** monkeys and **toco toucans** are abundant, as are endangered species like the tiny and aggressive **bush dog** and cats such as **ocelot** and **jaguarundi**. **Bare-faced currasows** (magnificent turkey-sized forest floor birds) can often be seen strutting around the pathways. Rarely seen small toucans such as the **chestnut-eared aracari** are relatively easy to spot here, flitting in and out of the trees.

For all its attractiveness, many of Bonito's prices are becoming almost offensively steep and many of the attractions would not be worth the entry ticket at half the price.

Arriving in Bonito

Getting there and around The *rodoviária* is on the edge of town. Several buses daily run to/from Campo Grande (five hours), Miranda (two to three hours) and Corumbá (five hours). Bonito town is a grid layout based around one principal street, Rua Coronel Pilad Rebuá, which extends for about 2 km. The town is easily negotiated on foot. ▸▸ *See Transport, page 62.*

Tourist information The tourist office: **Conselho Municipal de Turismo (COMTUR)** ⓘ *Rodovia Bonio, Guia Lopes da Laguna km1, T067-3255 2160, www.bonito- ms.com.br*, has limited information and staff do not speak English. The private website www.portalbonito.com.br is a more useful source of information. Prices in Bonito have risen sharply over the years, making the area prohibitively expensive for those on a budget. Local attractions can only be visited with prior booking through one of the town's

Fazendas in the southern Pantanal

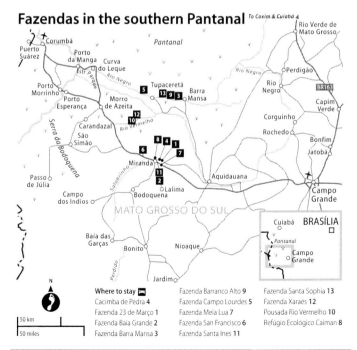

Where to stay 🛏
Cacimba de Pedra **4**
Fazenda 23 de Março **1**
Fazenda Baia Grande **2**
Fazenda Barra Mansa **3**

Fazenda Barranco Alto **9**
Fazenda Campo Lourdes **5**
Fazenda Meia Lua **7**
Fazenda San Francisco **6**
Fazenda Santa Ines **11**

Fazenda Santa Sophia **13**
Fazenda Xaraés **12**
Pousada Rio Vermelho **10**
Refúgio Ecológico Caiman **8**

numerous travel agents. With the exception of specialist activities like cave diving, all agents offer exactly the same products at exactly the same price, but only a few offer transport. Taxis to the sights are exorbitantly expensive; an alternative would be to hire a car. ▶ *See What to do, page 61.*

Best time to visit The number of visitors to Bonito is limited so pre-booking is essential during December and January, Carnaval, Easter and July; prices during these times are also very high. The wet season is in January and February; December to February are the hottest months; July and August coolest.

Places in Bonito

There are scores of different sights in Bonito and those sketched out below are a mere representative selection. The website www.bonito-ms.com.br has a full list, with pictures and links to each individual attraction's website.

Gruta Lagoa Azul ① *Rodovia para Tres Moros 22 km, daily 0700-1700, US$20*, is a cave with a lake 50 m long and 110 m wide, 75 m below ground level. The water's temperature is 20°C, and it is a jewel-like blue, as light from the opening is refracted through limestone and magnesium. Prehistoric animal bones have been found in the lake. The light is at its best in January and February, from 0700 to 0900, but is fine at other times. A 25-ha park surrounds the cave. The cave is filled with stalactites and stalagmites. It is reached via a very steep 294-step staircase which can be slippery in the rain and is completely unilluminated.

Nossa Senhora Aparecida cave has superb stalactites and stalagmites and can be visited, although there is no tourism infrastructure.

On the banks of the Rio Formoso, the **Balneário Municipal** ① *7 km on road to Jardim, US$4*, has changing rooms, toilets, camping, swimming in clear water and

Bonito

Where to stay 🛏
Albergue do Bonito 3
Canaã 2
Pira Miuna 6
Pousada Muito Bonito 1
Pousada Olho d'Água 4
São Jorge Hostel 5
Tapera 7

Restaurants 🍴
Cantinho do Peixe 3
Da Vovó 2
Mercado da Praça 5
Santa Esmeralda 1
Tapera 4

Bars & clubs 🍸
Bollicho 7
O Taboa 8

plenty of colourful fish to see. Strenuous efforts are made to keep the water and shore clean. The **Horminio waterfalls** ⓘ *US$1*, consist of eight falls, which are suitable for swimming. There's a bar and camping is possible. **Rafting** is also a popular activity. The 2½-hour trip combines floating peacefully downriver, swimming and shooting down the four waterfalls.

The **Aquário Natural** ⓘ *Estrada para Jardim 8 km and then 5.5 km of dirt road, daily 0900-1800, US$70 including lunch*, is a 600-m-long clear-water river lagoon filled with dourado and other fish and is formed by one of the springs of the Rio Formoso. This is the most child-friendly snorkelling in Bonito – easy and with almost no current.

It is possible to snorkel further along the **Rio Formoso** ⓘ *Estrada para Ilha do Padre 12 km, daily 0800-1700, US$28*, or float on rubber dinghies over gentle rapids.

One of the better value, and more peaceful tours involves birding and swimming or snorkelling in crystal-clear water from the springs of the **Rio Sucuri** ⓘ *Rodovia Bonito, Fazenda São Geraldo, Km 18, T067-3255 1030, daily 0900-1800, US$75 with lunch*, to its meeting with the Formoso, followed by horse riding or trail walking. Other tours include **Rio da Prata** (US$40), a beautiful spring with underground snorkelling for 2 km. There are also plenty of chances for walking along ecological trails, horse riding and fishing trips. The **fishing** season is from 1 March to 31 October. In late October and early November is the *piracema* (fish run). The fish return to the spawning grounds and hundreds can be seen jumping the falls.

Abismo Anhumas ⓘ *Fazenda Anhumas, Estrada para Campo dos Indios s/n, T067-3225 3313, US$210 (for abseiling and snorkelling) or US$310 (for rapelling and scuba diving)*, is another of Bonito's spectacular caves, filled with a glassy pool. The ticket gives visitors an abseil (of just a few metres) into the cave, followed by three to four hours snorkelling or scuba diving.

Bonito Aventura ⓘ *Estrada para Jardim 8 km, daily 0900-1800, US$28, including lunch*. This little reserve comprises a stand of pretty cerrado forest with many rodents like paca and agouti as well as capuchin monkeys and toco toucans in the trees. Trails cut through it to a clear-water river filled with fish.

Jardim

Jardim, reached by paved road (60 km from Bonito) could be an alternative base to Bonito for trips on clear-water rivers and visits to caves. There is far less infrastructure and consequently far fewer tourists and cheaper accommodation, restaurant and taxi prices. The town itself has a wide, tree-lined main street, a handful of hotels and basic café- restaurants. The official town website, www.jardim.ms.gov.br, has information and photos of what to see and do. The *rodoviária* has regular bus connections with Campo Grande and other towns (see Transport, page 63). From Bonito a road leads to **Porto Murtinho**, where a boat crosses to Isla Margarita in Paraguay (entry stamp available on the island).

Miranda → *For listings, see pages 56-64. Colour map 3, B2. Population: 23,000.*

This little farming town built around a now disused mill and a railway station lies some 200 km west of Campo Grande at the turn-off to Bonito. It has long been overlooked as a gateway to the Pantanal and Bonito, but is actually far closer to both than either Corumbá or Campo Grande. Miranda is also a real town, preoccupied more with its own local economy and culture than with tourism. It lies in the heart of indigenous Terena land and the communities have a large **cultural and arts centre** ① *at the entrance to town, Mon-Fri 0700-2200, Sat and Sun 0800-2200, free*, with panels on Terena history and arts and crafts for sale. Every October Miranda throws the spectacular **Festa do Homem Pantaneiro**: four days of rodeos, lassoing and general revelry that combine well with the water festival in Corumbá. For dates ask tour operators (see page 61). The crystal-clear river Salobrinho just outside town has great birdlife and a community of giant otters. There is a wonderful British girder bridge just west of town given as a gift to Brazil by King George V.

Arriving in Miranda The Campo Grande–Corumbá road crosses the Rio Miranda bridge (two service stations before it), then continues paved all the way to cross the Rio Paraguai. Miranda is served by numerous daily buses from Corumbá, Campo Grande and Bonito. There is a tourist booth just outside the *rodoviária*, opposite the **Zero Hora** bakery and supermarket. Rail services to Corumbá, onwards to Bolivia and eventually to Campo Grande are due to recommence in 2009. There is no tourist office but Aguas do Pantanal can provide information in English, see also www.mirandaemfoco.com. The town is tiny and can be walked from end to end in less than 10 minutes.

Miranda

N
Not to scale

Where to stay 🛏
Aguas do Pantanal **1**
Chalé **2**
Diogo **3**

Pantanal **4**

Restaurants 🍴
Cantina dell'Amore **1**

Zero Hora **2**

Trem do Pantanal

① Estação Ferroviaria s/n, T067-3384 6755, Sat-Sun 1 departure, US$38 or US$400 for a private cabin for up to 8 people, bookable only through tour operators like SAAB tourism or Brazil Nature Tours, see page 61.

Miranda is the terminus for the Trem do Pantanal. This is a tourist-designated diesel train which takes 13 hours to make the 220-km trip across the southwestern Pantanal from Campo Grande. The journey includes a two-hour stop for lunch in the tiny town of Aquidauana and breaks at stations to buy indigenous arts and crafts. There's little wildlife to see along the way – the occasional rhea strinding across the pasture, distant lakes filled with birds – but the journey is more comfortable and leisurely than on the bus.

Corumbá → *For listings, see pages 56-64. Colour map 3, B1. Phone code: 067. Population: 95,000.*

Situated on the south bank of the Rio Paraguai, by a broad bend, 15 minutes from the Bolivian border, Corumbá was long considered the best starting point for visiting the southern part of the Pantanal. And whilst many tour operators have now moved to Campo Grande, Corumbá still offers trips by boat or jeep and access to the major hotel and farm accommodation. Almost all the Campo Grande agencies have sub-offices here, those that don't can pick up from the city, and there are still a number of upmarket cruise companies along the waterfront. Corumbá is also the most attractive urban centre in the Pantanal – small enough to be intimate, with pretty Republican and colonial buildings along the waterfront and a very lively annual festival. It makes a pleasant one-night stopover between the Pantanal and Bolivia and is far more attractive than Campo Grande or Cuiabá.

Corumbá has a long history. The area where it lies was explored for the first time in 1524 by the Portuguese Aleixo Garcia and shortly after by the Spaniard Cabeza de Vaca whose name was prescient for a region that would come to depend on cattle. Both were in search of gold but found only Guiacurú warriors, who were among the fiercest and most effective fighters in Brazil, and who, like Crazy Horse, were finally defeated only through trickery. Their descendants are the modern-day Kadiweu, who still life in tiny numbers in the region.

By the 18th century the Paraguay river had become of strategic importance and skirmishes between Portuguese *bandeirantes* and the Spanish had become sufficiently tense to warrant the construction of the now ruined Forte Coimbra by Luiz Albuquerque de Mello Pereira e Cáceres, the Capitão-General of the Captaincy of Mato Grosso. This became the eastern outpost of Empire and the river became a frontier. A port grew up around the fort and the town's name became corrupted in common parlance from Coímbra to Corumbá. The town became an important Brazilian base in the Parguayan war of 1864-1870 and **Forte Junqueira** *① T067-3231 5828, Mon-Fri 0800-1100 and 1330-1630, R$2*, the city's second fort (which still stands and lies within the city limits), was built during the conflict.

From its earliest days Corumbá was as much a smuggling town as a military outpost. In the 1970s and 1980s it was so unprepossessing and potentially dangerous that the railway that ferried passengers in and out of Bolivia was popularly known as the Death Train. Whilst there is still illicit trade in Corumbá, Mato Grosso do Sul's prosperity has seen the town become more salubrious. The colonial buildings are freshly painted and there are even a smattering of smart restaurants. It is a pleasant town to spend a day or so; especially during the annual Festa de Nossa Senhora de Candelária when the streets are filled with processions and as much water is thrown about as in the Thai Songkran.

There are beautiful views from the quays out over the Paraguay river, especially at sunset, and some remnant colonial architecture. The compact streets include the spacious **Praça da Independência** and **Avenida General Rondon** (between Frei Mariano and 7 de Septembro), which has a palm-lined promenade that comes to life in the evenings. There is also hiking in the rugged Serra do Urucum hills to the south, where the world's greatest reserve of manganese is now being worked. There is a lively festival every October in Corumbá.

Arriving in Corumbá

Getting there and around The **airport** ⓘ *4 km west of town*, receives flights from Campo Grande. There is no public transport from the airport to town; you have to take a taxi (US$8). The **rodoviária** ⓘ *R Porto Carreiro at the south end of R Tiradentes*, is next to the

Corumbá

Where to stay 🛏
Aguas do Pantanal **2**
Angola **5**
Corumbá IYHA **7**
Nacional Palace & Pérola
do Pantanal Tours **1**

Premier **4**
Salette **6**
Santa Rita **3**

Restaurants 🍴
Almanara **3**

Avalom **6**
Laço de Ouro **5**
Panela Velha **4**
Peixeria de Lulú **2**
Verde Frutti **1**

Border essentials: Brazil–Bolivia

Corumbá (Brazil)–Puerto Suárez (Bolivia)

You will need to present a yellow fever vaccination certificate to enter Bolivia. If you arrive in Brazil without a yellow fever vaccination certificate, you may have to go to Rua 7 de Setembro, Corumbá, for an inoculation. There are money changers only at the border and in Quijarro (Bolivia).

Immigration Formalities are constantly changing, so check procedures in advance at the tourist office or *polícia federal*. At present there are 24 hour immigration posts on the Brazilian and Bolivian borders., and at the **Brazilian Polícia Federal** (Praça da República 37, Corumbá) at weekends 0800-1130 and 1330-1700. The visa must be obtained on the day of departure. If exiting Brazil in order to get a new visa, remember that exit and entry must not be on the same day.

Transport Leaving Brazil, take Canarinho city bus marked 'Fronteira' from the port end of Rua Antônio Maria Coelho to the Bolivian border (15 minutes, US$1.60), walk over the bridge to Bolivian immigration (blue building), then take a *colectivo* to Quijarro or Puerto Suárez. Taxis to the border cost US$3.

When entering Brazil from Quijarro, take a taxi or walk to the Bolivian border to go through formalities. Just past the bridge, on a small side street to the right, is the bus stop for Corumbá. Take a bus marked 'Fronteira' or 'Tamengo' to Praça da República (US$0.80, every 45 minutes 0630-1915); don't believe taxi drivers who say there is no bus. Taxi to the centre US$6. Brazilian immigration formalities are carried out at the *polícia federal*.

Into Bolivia Over the border from Corumbá are Arroyo Concepción, Puerto Quijarro and Puerto Suárez. From Puerto Quijarro a a 650-km railway runs to Santa Cruz daily (www.ferroviariaoriental.com). There is a road of sorts. A better road route is from Cáceres to San Matías, then to San Ignacio (see page 69). There are internal flights from Puerto Suárez.

railway station. A city bus to Praça da República costs US$0.80. Taxis are extortionate, but moto-taxis charge only US$0.65.

Safety Over the last five years Corumbá has become increasingly unsafe. Be careful here, especially after dark.

Tourist information The municipal tourist office, **Sematur** ① *R América 969, T067-231 7336*, provides general information and city maps. The combination of economic hard times and drug running make the city unsafe late at night.

Climate Corumbá is hot (particularly between September and January), with 70% humidity; June and July are cooler. Mosquitoes can be a real problem from December to February.

Mato Grosso do Sul and the Southern Pantanal listings

For hotel and restaurant price codes and other relevant information, see pages 9-12.

🛏 Where to stay

Campo Grande *p45, map p47*
The better hotels lie near the city centre. There are lots of cheaper hotels in the streets around the *rodoviária* so it is easy to leave bags in the *guarda volumes* and shop around. This area is not safe at night.

$$$$ Jandaia, R Barão do Rio Branco 1271, T067-3316 7700, www.jandaia.com.br. The city's best hotel, aimed at a business market. Modern well-appointed rooms (with Wi-Fi) in a tower. The best are above the 10th floor. Pool, gym and some English spoken.

$$$-$$ Advanced, Av Calógeras 1909, T067-3321 5000, www.hoteladvanced.com.br. Clean, spacious, spartan rooms with en suites and boiler-heated showers, in a 1980s block with a very small pool. Cheaper with fan.

$$$-$$ Internacional, R Alan Kardec 223, T067- 3384 4677, www.hotel internacional.com.br. Small but comfortable rooms with a/c or fans and flatpack furniture, or newly renovated suites with smart bathrooms in slate and tile and cable TV. Pool and restaurant. Quiet street near the *rodoviária*.

$$ Concord, Av Calógeras 1624, T067-3384 3081, www.hotelconcord.com.br. A standard town hotel with a small pool and renovated a/c rooms with modern fittings.

$$ Nacional, R Dom Aquino 610, T067-3383 2461, hotelnacional@ig.com.br. Quiet, well-kept hotel with simple rooms with fans and proper mattresses. Some en suites. TV room and internet.

$$-$ Hostel Campo Grande, R Joaquim Nabuco 185, opposite old rodoviária, T3042 0508. Simple, musty little rooms with saggy foam mattresses and frayed bathrooms. Laundry, kitchen, pool, internet; reception open 24 hrs. **Ecological Expeditions** offer

Pantanal trips from their office next door. Low price per person.

$$-$ Hostel Santa Clara, R Vitor Meirelles 125, T3384 0583, www.pantanalsanta clara.com.br. A pleasant hostel in a converted town house with a large garden five minutes from the new rodoviária. Free airport pick-up, wifi, kitchen, tour agency a dn a/c doubles and dorms.

$ Iguaçu, R Dom Aquino 761, T067-3322 4621, www.hoteliguacu.com.br. Very popular well-kept hotel next to the *rodoviária* with smart, simple a/c rooms with cable TV. Good breakfast.

Ponta Porã *p48*
Brazilian hotels include breakfast in tariff; Paraguayan ones do not.

$$$-$$ Barcelona, R Guia Lopes 45, T067-3437 2500. Simple but well kept, with a/c or fan-cooled rooms. Bar and sauna.

$$ Alvorada, Av Brasil 2977, T067-3431 5866. With a good café, close to post office, good value but often full.

$$-$ Internacional, R Internacional 1267, T067-3431 1243. Cheaper without a/c. Hot water, good breakfast. Recommended.

$ Dos Viajantes, R Albino Torraca 591, T067-3421 8817, across park opposite the railway station. Very basic and only for those on the tightest budget.

Bonito *p48, map p50*
$$$ Pira Miuna, R Luís da Costa Leite 1792, T067-3255 1058, www.piramiunahotel. com.br. Huge, ugly brick building with the most comfortable a/c rooms in the centre and a large pool area with jacuzzis and a bar.

$$$ Pousada Olho d'Água, Rod Três Morros, Km 1, T067-3255 1430, www.pousadaolhodagua.com.br. Comfortable accommodation in fan-cooled cabins set in an orchard next to a small lake. Horse riding, bike rental, solar-powered hot water and great food from the vegetable garden. Recommended.

$$$ Tapera, Estrada Ilha do Padre, Km 10, on the hill above the Shell station on the road to Jardim, T/F067-3255 1700, www.tapera hotel.com.br. Peaceful location with fine views and cool breezes. Very comfortable, but own transport an advantage.

$$-$ Albergue do Bonito, R Lúcio Borralho 716, Vila Donária, T/F067-3255 1462, www.bonitohostel.com.br. IYHA youth hostel. A well-run hostel with a travel agency, pool, kitchen and laundry facilities. English spoken, very friendly. Price per person for dorms.

$ Pousada Muito Bonito, R Col Pilad Rebuá 1448, T/F067-3255 1645, www.muito bonito.com.br. Price per person in en suites or dorm-style rooms with bunk beds, all with a nice shared patio. Clean, excellent and with helpful owners and a tour operator (Mario Doblack at the tour office speaks English, French and Spanish). Price includes breakfast.

Camping
Camping Rio Formoso, Rodovia Bonito/Guia Lopes da Laguna Km 06, T067-9284 5994, www.campingrio formoso.com.br. With space for 60 tents.

Miranda *p51, map p52*
$$ Hotel Chalé, Av Barão do Rio Branco 685, T067-242 1216, hotelchale@star5.com.br. Plain a/c motel-like rooms with tiled floors and en suites, and a pool.

$$ Pantanal Hotel, Av Barão do Rio Branco 609, T067-3242 1068. Standard town hotel with pool and well-maintained a/c rooms with en suite, set along a gloomy corridor.

$$ Pantanal Ranch Mandovi, BR 262 km 554, T9686 9064, www.pantanalranch mandovi.com. Lovely rustic guest house set in forested gardens and run by a Kadiweu indigenous Pantaneiro and his Swiss wife. Great food, lovely atmosphere, many birds (including Hyacinth macaws) and some of

the best tours in the Pantanal. Full board available and camping area (**$**).

$ Diogo, Av Barão do Rio Branco s/n, T067-242 1468. Very simple but well-kept doubles, triples and quadruples, some with a/c.

Fazendas around Miranda
Prices below include accommodation, all food and at least 2 guided trips per day. Standard packages include jeep trips, trail walks, horse riding, boat trips (where the *fazenda* has a river) and night safaris. They do not always include transfer from Miranda or the Buraco da Onca and this should be checked when booking. Unless otherwise indicated the standard of wildlife guiding will be poor, with common familial or generic names known only for animals and little awareness of species diversity or numbers. Keen birdwatchers should request a specialist birding guide through their tour operator or *fazenda*. Also take a good pair of binoculars and some field guides. The following *fazendas* can be booked through **Brazil Nature Tours** in Campo Grande, page 61, or **Aguas do Pantanal Turismo** in Miranda, page 62. Tours are the same price even if you are on your own, but there are almost always other guests.

$$$$ Refúgio Ecológico Caiman, 36 km from Miranda, T011-3706 1800, www.caiman.com.br. The most comfortable, stylish accommodation in the Pantanal in a hotel reminiscent of a Mexican hacienda. Tours and guiding are excellent. Part of the **Roteiros de Charme** group (see page 10). Open sporadically only. Check website.

$$$ Cacimba de Pedra, Estr Agachi, T067-9982 4655, www.cacimbadepedra.com.br. A Jacaré caiman farm and *pousada* in beautiful dry deciduous forest cut by trails and dotted with lakes. A/c rooms are simple but spruce and sit in front of an inviting pool. The forest is abundant with wildlife. There is a hyacinth macaw nest on the farm and tapir sightings are common.

$$$ Fazenda Baia Grande, Estr La Lima, Km 19, T067-3382 4223, www.fazendabaia grande.com.br. Very comfortable a/c rooms set around a pool in a bougainvillea and ipê-filled garden. The fazenda is surrounded by savannah and stands of cerrado broken by large lakes. The owner, Alex, is very friendly, eager to please and enthusiastic.

$$$ Fazenda San Francisco, turn off BR-262 30 km west of Miranda, T3242 3333, www.fazendasanfrancisco.tur.br. One of the most popular and heavily visited ranches in the Pantanal with large day groups, especially at weekends, and simple rustic a/c cabins gathered around a pool in a garden filled with rheas. Food and guides are excellent.

$$$ Fazenda 23 de Março, T067-3321 4737, www.fazenda23de marco.com.br. Simple rustic fazenda with only 4 rooms near Miranda in Aquidauna. There are programmes orientated to budget travellers, and **Centrapan**, a centre for the preservation of Pantanal culture, where visitors can learn to lasso, ride a bronco and turn their hand to other Pantanal cowboy activities.

Fazendas on the Estrada Parque

The Estrada Parque is a dirt road that cuts through the Pantanal near Miranda – running in a right angle through the wetlands and eventually arriving in Corumbá town. See map, page 49.

$$$$ Fazenda Xaraés, www.xaraes.com.br. One of the most luxurious fazendas, with a pool, tennis court, sauna, airstrip and modest but well-appointed a/c rooms in cream and terracotta. The immediate environs have been extensively cleared, but there are some wild areas of savannah and cerrado nearby and there are giant otters in the neighbouring Rio Abodrai.

$$$$-$$$ Fazenda Barra Mansa, www.hotel barramansa.com.br. One of the better lodges in the region in a wild area right on the banks of the Rio Negro and between 2 large tracts of wetland. Like all the Rio Negro fazendas it is famous for its jaguars. Specialist guiding is available on request; be sure to stipulate this in advance. The farm also offers sport fishing, horse riding and canoe trips on the river. Accommodation for up to 16 is in rustic a/c rooms with hammocks. There is a small library of field guides at the fazenda.

$$$$-$$$ Fazenda Barranco Alto, Caixa postal 109, Aquidauana, Mato Grosso do Sul, T067-3241 4047, www.fazendabarranco alto.com.br. A beautiful, remote large ranch on the banks of the Rio Negro and owned and run by and agronomist and his biologist wife. Along with the neighbouring **Fazenda Rio Negro**, it is one of the oldest fazendas in the Pantanal with farm buildings dating from the first half of the 20th century. The surrounding area has stands of cerrado set in seasonally flooded savannah cut by the river. Guiding is good but stipulate your interest in wildlife in advance, especially if you are a birder.

$$$Fazenda Santa Clara, Estrada Parque s/n, T3384 0583, www.pantanalsanta clara.com.br. The best comfortable budget option for staying in a ranch house in the Southern Pantanal, on the banks of the Rio Alobrão (where there's a community of giant otters), and with a pool, games areas, double rooms and dorms, full transfers from Campo Grande, full board and tours included. Well-organized and well-run.

Corumbá p53, map p54

There are hostels around the bus station, however this is a 10-min walk from the centre of town where most of the hotels, restaurants and tour agencies are found.

$$$-$$ Aguas do Pantanal Palace hotel, R Dom Aquino Corrêa 1457, T067-3234 8800, www.aguasdopantanalhotel.com.br. The smartest in town together with the **Nacional Palace**, with a/c rooms in a 1980s tower, a pool and sauna.

$$$-$$ Nacional Palace, R América 936, T067-3234 6000, www.hnacional.com.br.

Smart, modern a/c rooms, a decent pool and parking.

$$-$ Salette, R Delamaré 893, T067-3231 6246. Cheap and cheerful with a range of rooms, the cheapest with fans and shared bathrooms. Recommended.

$ HI Corumbá, R Colombo 1419, T067-3231 1005, www.corumbahostel.com.br. A newly opened, well-equipped modern hostel with helpful staff and a pool. A/c or fan-cooled rooms and dorms.

Restaurants

Campo Grande *p45, map p47*
Local specialities include *caldo de piranha* (soup), *chipa* (Paraguayan cheese bread, sold on the streets, delicious when hot) and the local liqueur, *pequi com caju*, which contains *cachaça* (sugar-cane rum). There are many cheap restaurants around the *rodoviária* and many others in the **Shopping Campo Grande** mall.

$$$ Comitiva Pantaneira, R Dom Aquino 2221, T067-3383 8799. Hearty, tasty and very meaty regional dishes served by waiters in cowboy gear or as a buffet. Lunchtime only.

$$$ Gaúcho Gastão, R 14 de Julho 775, T067- 3384 4326. The best *churrascaria* in town, famous for its beef. Comfortable. Lunch only.

$$ Cantina Romana, R da Paz, 237, T067-3324 9777. Established for more than 20 years, Italian dishes, salads and a lunchtime buffet, good atmosphere.

$$-$ Sabor en Quilo, R Barão do Rio Branco 1118 and R Dom Aquino 1786, T067-3383 3911. Lunchtime only. Self-service per kilo restaurants with plenty of choice including sushi on Sat.

$ Morada dos Bais, Av Noroeste, 5140, corner with Afonso Pena, behind tourist office. Brazilian and Italian dishes, snacks and coffee served in a pretty courtyard, Lunchtime only.

Bonito *p48, map p50*
$$$-$$ Santa Esmeralda, R Col Pilad Rebuá 1831. Respectable Italian food in one of the few a/c dining rooms.

$$ Tapera, R Col Pilad Rebuá 480, T067-3255 1110. Good, home-grown vegetables, breakfast, lunch, pizzas, meat and fish dishes, opens 1900 for the evening meal.

$ Da Vovó, R Sen F Muller 570, T067-3255 2723. A great per kilo restaurant serving Minas and local food all cooked in a traditional wood-burning aga. Plenty of veg and salads.

$ Mercado da Praça, R 15 Novembro 376, T067-3255 2317. The cheapest in town. A snack bar housed in the local supermarket, offering sandwiches and juices 0600-2400.

Miranda *p51, map p52*
$ Zero Hora, Av Barão do Rio Branco at the *rodoviária*, T067-3242 1330. 24-hr snack bar, provision shop and, at the back, there's an average but good-value per kilo restaurant, with its own private waterfall.

Corumbá *p53, map p54*
Local specialities include *peixadas corum-baenses*, a variety of fish dishes prepared with the catch of the day; as well as ice cream, liquor and sweets made of *bocaiúva*, a small yellow palm fruit, in season Sep-Feb. There is a range of decent restaurants in R Frei Mariano including a number of *churrascarias* and pasta restaurants. You'll find plenty of good simple fish restaurant bars on the waterfront.

$$ Laço de Ouro, R Frei Mariano 556, T067-3231 7371. Very popular fish restaurant with a lively atmosphere and tables spilling out onto the street. Similar crowd to **Avalom**.

$ Panela Velha, R 15 de Novembro 156, T067-3232 5650. Popular lunchtime restaurant with a decent, cheap all-you-can-eat buffet.

$ Verde Frutti, R Delamaré 1164, T067-3231 3032. A snack bar with a wide variety of juices and great, ice-cold *açai na tigela*.

☾ Bars and clubs

Campo Grande *p45, map p47*
The best of the chic bars are on **R Afonso Pena**, beyond the monument, and along the streets to the north of Afonso Pena.
Choppão, R Dom Aquino 2331, T067-3383 9471. Lively open-sided bar with live music from Thu to Sat.
Morada dos Bais, see Restaurants, above. Restaurant and *choperia*, live music in the courtyard, daily from 2030, free.
Mostarda, Av Afonso Pena 3952, T067-3026 8469. Popular 20- and 30-something bar which is always lively after 2200 and hosts live music at weekends.

Clubs

There are a number of clubs open Thu-Sat, including **Tango**, R Cândido Mariano 2181, www.tangobar.com.br, and for something a little more alternative try **Bazar** or **Garagem**, R Doutor Temístocles 94.

Bonito *p48, map p50*
O Taboa, R Col Pilad Rebuá 1837, T067-3255 1862. The liveliest in town with occasional bands and good caipirinhas and *chopp*.

✿ Festivals

Corumbá *p53, map p54*
2 Feb Festa de Nossa Senhora da Candelária, Corumbá's patron saint, all offices and shops are closed.
24 Jun Festa do Arraial do Banho de São João, fireworks, parades, traditional food, processions and the main event – the bathing of the image of the saint in the Rio Paraguai.
21 Sep Corumbá's anniversary, includes a Pantanal **fishing festival** held on the eve.

Mid-Oct Festival Pantanal das Águas, with street parades featuring giant puppets, street dancing and occasional water fights.

◎ Shopping

Campo Grande *p45, map p47*
Local native crafts, including ceramics, tapestry and jewellery, are of good quality. A local speciality is *os bugres da conceição* (squat wooden statues covered in moulded wax). Very good selections are found at **Casa do Artesão**, Av Calógeras 2050, on the corner with Av Afonso Pena. Mon-Fri 0800-2000, Sat 0800-1200. Also try: **Barroarte**, Av Afonso Pena 4329, and **Arte do Pantanal**, Av Afonso Pena 1743. There is a market (*Feira Livre*) on Wed and Sat. **Shopping Campo Grande**, Av Afonso Pena 4909, www.shoppingcampo grande.com.br, is the largest shopping mall in town, on its eastern edge.

Corumbá *p53, map p54*
Shops tend to open early and close by 1700.
Casa do Artesão, R Dom Aquino 405, in a converted prison. Mon-Fri 0800-1200, 1400-1800, Sat 0800-1200, good selection of handicrafts and a small bookshop.
CorumbArte, Av Gen Rondon 1011. Good silk-screen T-shirts with Pantanal motifs.
Frutal, R 13 de Junho 538. Open 0800-2000. Supermarket.
Livraria Corumbaense, R Delamaré 1080. Useful for state maps.
Ohara, Dom Aquino 621, corner Antônio João. Supermarket.

▲ What to do

Wildlife guides for the Pantanal

See also tour operators and guides for the northern Pantanal, page 80.
Alyson is a Londrina-based birding guide who works with **Neblina Forest Tours** (www.neblinaforest.com); available through **Fazenda San Francisco**.

Juan Mazar Barnett, T+54 (0)11-4312 6345, www.seriemanaturetours.com. Very experienced Buenos Aires-based birding guide and editor of *Cotinga* magazine. Expert on *chaco* and Pantanal birds. Book well ahead; expensive.

Campo Grande *p45, map p47*
City Tour, T067-3321 0800, or through the Campo Grande Pantanal visitor centre and most larger hotels. Half-day tours of the city's sights including the Museu Dom Bosco and the Parque das Nações Indígenas.

Tours to the southern Pantanal
Brazil Nature Tours, R Guia Lopes 150, 1st floor, T067-3042 4659, www.brazilnature tours.com. Booking agents for nature-based tours throughout Brazil, flights, buses and the *fazendas* of the Pantanal, north and south.

Ecological Expeditions, R Joaquim Nabuco 185, T067-3321 0505, www.ecologicalexpeditions.com.br; with another office in Corumbá, see below. Attached to the youth hostel at the bus station. Offers budget camping trips and lodge-based trips in **Nhecolândia** (sleeping bag needed) for 3, 4 or 5 days ending in Corumbá. The 1st day, which involves travel to the Buraco da Piranha, is free.

Impacto, R 7 de Setembro 1090, T067-3325 1333, www.impactotour.com.br. Very helpful Pantanal and Bonito tour operator established over 10 years. Prices vary according to standard of accommodation; a wide range is offered. 2-day packages for 2 people US$190-600. Transfers and insurance included. English spoken.

Bonito and around *p48, map p50*
There is very little to choose between agencies in Bonito. English speakers are hard to come by. We list only those who also offer transport or a specialist service such as cave diving.

Impacto, R Col Pilad Rebuá 1515, T067-3255 1414. English-speaking staff. Can be pre- booked through their efficient head office in Campo Grande or through **Aguas do Pantanal Turismo** in Miranda (see below).

City Tour, R Col Pilad Rebuá 1515, T067-3255 1414. English-speaking staff. Can be pre-booked through their efficient head office in Campo Grande or through **Aguas do Pantanal Turismo** in Miranda (see below).

Ygarapé, R Col Pilad Rebuá 1956, T067-3255 1733, www.ygarape.com.br. English spoken. PDSE accredited cave diving.

Miranda *p51, map p52*

Tours to the southern Pantanal
Both of the operators below can organize accommodation during the **Festa do Homem Pantaneiro** (see Festivals above).

Explore Pantanal, R Dr Alexandre 305, Miranda, T067-3242 4310, T067-9638 3520, www.explore pantanal.com. Run by a Kadiweu indigenous guide and his Swiss partner, with many years of experience. Very good English, German, French, Spanish and Italian and decent Hebrew. Great for small groups who want to get off the beaten track. A range of excursions, including fascinating stays with indigenous people in the Pantanal. Trips to Bonito (including pre-arranged transport), camping tours and day tours. Prices are competitive with budget operators in Campo Grande and Corumbá. For best rates book ahead.

Corumbá *p53, map p54*

Tours to the southern Pantanal
Ecological Expeditions, R Antônio Maria Coelho 78. Main office in Campo Grande.

Mutum Turismo, R Frei Mariano 17, T067-3231 1818, www.mutumturismo.com.br. Cruises and upmarket tours (mostly aimed at the Brazilian market) and help with airline, train and bus reservations.

Pantanal fishing and river cruises
Pérola do Pantanal, Nacional Palace (see Where to stay), T067-3231 1470, www.peroladopantanal.com.br. Fishing and 'eco' tours on their large river boat, *Kalypso*, with options of added jeep trips on the Estrada Parque.

⊘ Transport

Campo Grande *p45, map p47*
Air The airport is 7 km from the city centre; to get there take city bus No 158, which stops outside the airport; taxi US$6.

As ever, the cheapest flights are available on line. Agencies in the city (many offices in front of the *rodoviária*) will book online and charge to credit cards. Campo Grande has flights to **Brasília**, **Cuiabá**, **Manaus**, **Porto Alegre**, **Santa Cruz** (Bolivia), **São Paulo**, **Porto Velho**, **Corumbá**, **Goiânia**, **Londrina**, **Belo Horizonte**, **Campinas**, **Corumbá**, **Cuiabá**, **Curitiba**, **Salvador** and many others.

Airlines include: **Avianca**, www.Avianca. com.br; **Azul**, www.voeazul.com.br; **GOL**, www.voe gol.com.br; **TAM**, www.tam. com.br; **TRIP**, www.voetrip. com.br.

Bus Town buses leave from the R Vasconcelos Fernandes end of the *rodoviária*, while state and interstate buses leave from the R Joaquim Nabuco end.

To **São Paulo**, US$80, 14 hrs, 9 buses daily, 1st at 0800, last at 2400, 3 *leito* buses US$105. To **Cuiabá**, US$45, 10 hrs, 12 buses daily, *leito* at 2100 and 2200, US$55. To **Brasília**, US$80, 23 hrs at 1000 and 2000. To **Goiânia**, with São Luís at 1100, 2000, 15 hrs on 1900 service, US$65, others 24 hrs, but only US$5 cheaper. **Rio de Janeiro**, US$80, 21 hrs, 4 buses daily, *leito* at 1540, US$100. To **Belo Horizonte**, 22 hrs, US$80.

To **Corumbá**, with Andorinha, 8 daily from 0600, 6 hrs, US$35. Campo Grande– Corumbá buses connect with those from Rio and São Paulo, similarly those from Corumbá through to Rio and São Paulo. To **Ponta Porã**, 5 hrs, 9 buses daily, US$15. To **(Queiroz)**, US$14. Beyond Dourados is **Mundo Novo**, from where buses go to **Ponta Porã** (0530) and to **Porto Frajelli** (very frequent). From Mundo Novo, ferries for cars and passengers go to **Guaíra** for US$3. Twice daily direct service to **Foz do Iguaçu** (17 hrs) with **Integração**, 1600, US$45; also to **Cascavel**, US$40. To **Pedro Juan Caballero** (Paraguay), del Amambay company, 0600, US$21. **Amambay** goes every Sun morning to **Asunción** (Paraguay).

Car hire Hertz, Av Afonso Pena 2620 and airport, T067-3383 5331. **Locagrande**, Av Afonso Pena 466, T067-3721 3282. **Localiza**, Av Afonso Pena 318, T067-3382 8786, and at the airport, along with various others T0800-992000. **Unidas**, Av Afonso Pena 829, T067-3384 5626, at airport, T067-3363 2145.

Ponta Porã *p48*
Bus To **Campo Grande**, 9 a day 0100-2130, 4 hrs, US$15.

Bonito *p48, map p50*
Bus To **Campo Grande**, 0530, US$15, 5½-6 hrs. Buses use the MS-345, with a stop at **Autoposto Santa Cruz**, Km 60 (all types of fuel, food and drinks available). Several daily buses to **Miranda**. Some buses to Corumbá and Campo Grande buses call in here; check at the *rodoviária*. There is a bus that runs Corumbá– Miranda–Bonito–Jardim–Ponta Porã, Mon-Sat, leaves either end at 0600, arriving Bonito at 1230 for **Ponta Porã** or 1300 for **Miranda**; for **Campo Grande** it's also possible to change in Jardim (1400 for 1700 bus) or Miranda, which have better connections. The fare to **Corumbá** is US$15. There are also connections on the 1230 route to **Bela Vista** at 2000 or **Asunción**

(Paraguay) and **Col Oviedo** (Paraguay). Ticket office opens at 1200.

Jardim *p51*
Bus To **Campo Grande**, 0530, 1200, 1600 and 2 at night, US$25, 5 hrs. To **Bonito** (US$6.50), **Miranda** and **Corumbá** at 1130. To **Dourados**, 0600. To **Bela Vista** (Paraguayan border) 0200, 1030, 1500, 1930. To **Porto Murtinho**, 0010 and 1530 (bus from Bonito connects). To **Ponta Porã**, 0600, 1500; Sun only at 1400 to **São Paulo**.

Miranda *p51, map p52*
Bus To **Campo Grande**, 12 a day (2- 3 hrs), US$25. To **Corumbá**; 10 daily (3-4 hrs), US$15. To **Bonito**, 1 daily (2-3 hrs), US$15 at 1700.

Corumbá *p53, map p54*
Air The airport is 3 km from the city centre; taxi US$6 or there is an infrequent bus. Flights to **Brasília** and **Campo Grande** with **Tam**, www.tam.com.br, and **Trip**, www.voetrip.com.br.

Boat The *Acurí*, a luxury vessel, sails between Corumbá and **Cáceres** once a week, US$600 including return by air. For further details, see Cáceres transport, page 83.

Bus Andorinha services to all points east. To **Campo Grande**, 7 hrs, US$25, 13 buses daily 0630-2400, interesting journey ('an excursion in itself'); take an early bus for a chance of seeing wildlife, connections from Campo Grande to all parts of Brazil. To **São Paulo** direct, 22 hrs, US$90, 1100 and 1500, confirm bus times in advance as these change (T067-3231 2033). To **Rio de Janeiro** direct, 30 hrs, US$105, daily 1100. **Cruzeiro do Sul** operates the route south to the **Paraguayan border**. To **Ponta Porã**, 12 hrs, US$40, Bonito (6 hrs, US$20) and Jardim

(9 hrs, US$25). At least 4 daily to **Miranda**. Mon-Sat at 0600; ticket office open 0500-0600 only, at other times call T067-3231 2383.

Car hire Localiza, airport and R Cabral 2064, T067-231 6000. **Unidas**, R Frei Mariano 633, T/F067-231 3124.

❶ Directory

Campo Grande *p45, map p47*
Banks Banco do Brasil, 13 de Maio and Av Afonso Pena, open 1100-1600, charges commission US$10 for cash, US$20 for TCs, regardless of amount exchanged. Visa ATMs at **Bradesco**, 13 de Maio and Av Afonso Pena; at **HSBC**, R 13 de Maio 2837; and at **Banco 24 horas**, R Maracaju, on corner with 13 de Junho. Also at R Dom Aquino and Joaquim Nabuco. **Overcash Câmbio**, R Rui Barbosa 2750, Mon-Fri 1000-1600. **Embassies and consulates** Bolivia, R João Pedro de Souza 798, T067-382 2190. **Paraguay**, R 26 Agosto 384, T067-324 4934. **Internet** Cyber Café **Iris**, Av Afonso Pena 1975, and **Cyber Café**, R Alan Kardec 374, T067-3384 5963 near the Hotel Turis. Also in the IYHA. **Medical services** Yellow and dengue fevers are both present in Mato Grosso do Sul; the former only in very remote areas. There is a clinic at the railway station, but it's not very hygienic, best to get your immunizations at home. **Post office** On corner of R Dom Aquino and Av Calógeras 2309, and Barão do Rio Branco on corner of Ernesto Geisel, both locations offer fax service, US$2.10 per page within Brazil. **Telephone** Telems, R 13 de Maio and R 15 de Novembro, daily 0600-2200.

Ponta Porã *p48*
Banks Banco do Brasil changes TCs. Many in the centre of town (but on Sun change money in hotels). **Bradesco** has a Visa ATM.

Bonito *p48, map p50*

Banks The town has a **Bradesco** bank for Visa ATM on Av Coronel Pilão Rebuá, 535. **Banco do Brasil**, R Luís da Costa Leite 2279 for Visa. Some hoteliers and taxi drivers may change money. **Post office** R Col Pilad Rebuá. **Telephone** Santana do Paraíso.

Jardim *p51*

Banks Elia, a taxi driver, will change money; ask around.

Miranda *p51, map p52*

Banks The town has both a **Bradesco** and a **Banco do Brasil**. **Internet** Star Informatica, R Francisco Rebúa 149, T06/-3242 2100.

Corumbá *p53, map p54*

Banks **Banco do Brasil**, R 13 de Junho 914, ATM. **HSBC**, R Delamaré 1068, ATM. **HSBC**, R Delamaré 1068, ATM. **Câmbio Mattos**, R 15 de Novembro 140, Mon-Fri 0800-1700, good rates for US$ cash, US$5 commission on TCs. **Câmbio Rau**, R 15 de Novembro 212, Mon-Fri 0800-1700, Sat 0900-1200, cash only, good rates. **Embassies and consulates Bolivia**, R Antônio Maria Coelho 881, T067-231 5605, Mon-Fri 0700-1100, 1500-1730. A fee is charged to citizens of those countries that require a visa. A yellow fever vaccination certificate is also required. **Internet Pantanalnet**, R América 430, US$2.50 per hr. **Laundry** Apae, R 13 de Junho 1377, same day service. **Post office** Main office at R Delamaré 708, fax service. Branch at R 15 de Novembro 229. **Telephone** R Dom Aquino 951, near Praça da Independência, daily 0700-2200. To phone Quijarro/Puerto Suárez, Bolivia, costs slightly more than a local call; dial 214 + the Bolivian number.

Mato Grosso and the Northern Pantanal

Mato Grosso, immediately to the north of Mato Grosso do Sul, shares the Pantanal with that state and has equally well-developed tourism facilities. Although there are just as many opportunities for seeing wildlife, trips to the Pantanal near the state capital, Cuiabá, tend to be more upmarket than those leaving from Corumbá in Mato Grosso do Sul. The state also has abundant though rapidly depleting areas of Amazon forest; Alta Floresta, in the north, has an excellent birdwatching and wildlife lodge and one of the Amazon's most comfortable lodges, the Jardim da Amazônia, lies in the middle of vast fields of soya to Alta Floresta's southwest. The much-vaunted Chapada dos Guimarães hills, near Cuiabá, afford good light walking and birdwatching, although the natural landscape has been greatly damaged by farming and development.

Cuiabá → *For listings, see pages 76-83. Colour map 3, A2. Phone code: 065. Population: 470,000.*

An important starting point for trips into the Pantanal, Cuiabá, a state capital, is an ordered and increasingly wealthy city; rich on soya from the vast plantations to the north. There are few sights of more than a passing interest, but the city has a number of leafy *praças* leading it to be called the 'Cidade Verde' (green city) by Matogrossenses. Cuiabá is in reality two twinned cities – separated by the sluggish Rio Cuiabá, an upper tributary of the Rio Paraguai – **Cuiabá** on the east bank of the river, and **Várzea Grande** on the west. They vie with Teresina in Piauí and Corumbá in Matto Grosso do Sul as the hottest cities in Brazil, with temperatures pushing up to the high 40s in the Antipodean summer months. The coolest months are June, July and August in the dry season.

Arriving in Cuiabá
Getting there Flights arrive at **Marechal Rondon airport** ⓘ *Av João Ponce de Arruda, s/n, Várzea Grande, T065-3614 2500, 10 km from the centre*, from Alta Floresta, Brasília, Campo Grande, São Paulo, Rio and Salvador, amongst others. There are ATMs outside the airport, as well as a post office, car hire booths and **Sedtur** office. To get to the centre, take any white Tuiuiú bus (the name will be written on the side), from in front of the airport to Avenida Tenente Coronel Duarte. Taxis cost US$20. Interstate buses arrive at the **rodoviária** ⓘ *north of the centre at R Jules Rimet, Bairro Alvorada*. Town buses stop at the entrance of the *rodoviária*. ▶▶ *See Transport, page 82.*

Getting around Many bus routes have stops in the vicinity of Praça Ipiranga. Bus Nos 501 or 505 ('Universidade') to the university museums and zoo (ask for 'Teatro') leave from Avenida Tenente Coronel Duarte by Praça Bispo Dom José, a triangular park just east of Praça Ipiranga.

Tourist information Sedtur ① *R Marechal Rondon, Jardim Aeroporto, Várzea Grande and with a smaller office at R Ricardo Franca at Voluntarios da Patria, T065-3613 9300, Mon-Fri 0900-1800, www.sedtur.mt.gov.br*, provides maps and general information on hotels and car hire and has a website in English. Staff are friendly and speak English and Spanish. They are very helpful in settling disputes with local tour companies.

Places in Cuiabá

The most pleasant public space in Cuiabá is the lush **Praça da República** which is surrounded by a cluster of imposing buildings and dotted with sculptures and shady

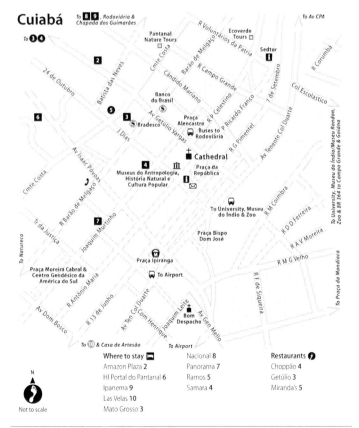

Cuiabá

Where to stay 🛏		Restaurants 🍴
Amazon Plaza 2	Nacional 8	Choppão 4
HI Portal do Pantanal 6	Panorama 7	Getúlio 3
Ipanema 9	Ramos 5	Miranda's 5
Las Velas 10	Samara 4	
Mato Grosso 3		

N
Not to scale

trees. Other pedestrian shopping streets and further squares lead off the *praça*. The brutalist façade of the **cathedral**, flanked by two functionalist clock towers, dominates the square. Until the late 1960s a beautiful 18th-century baroque church stood here but this was demolished to make way for the current building in a sweep of modernization that saw almost all the city's colonial charm destroyed.

On **Praça Ipiranga**, at the junction of avenidas Isaac Póvoas and Tenente Coronel Duarte, a few blocks southwest of the central squares, there are market stalls and an iron bandstand from Huddersfield in the UK, or Hamburg in Germany, depending on which story you believe. There is live acoustic music on Thursday and Friday on the **Praça da Mandioca**, a small square just east of the centre.

On a hill beyond the square is the extraordinary church of **Bom Despacho**, built in the style of Notre Dame. It is best viewed from afar as it is sadly run down and not open to visitors. In front of the Assembléia Legislativa on Praça Moreira Cabral, is a point marking the **Geodesic Centre of South America** (see also under Chapada dos Guimarães, below).

The rather dusty **Museus de Antropologia, História Natural e Cultura Popular** ① *Fundação Cultural de Mato Grosso, Praça da República 151, Mon-Fri 0800-1730, US$0.50*, are worth a look. There are interesting historical photos, a contemporary art gallery, indigenous weapons, archaeological finds and pottery. The section of stuffed wildlife from the Pantanal is disturbingly compelling.

At the entrance to the Universidade de Mato Grosso by the swimming pool, 10 minutes by bus from the centre, is the small **Museu do Índio/Museu Rondon** ① *T065-3615 8489, www.ufmt.br/ichs/museu_rondon/museu_rondon.html, Tue-Sun 0800-1100, 1330-1700, US$1*, with artefacts from tribes mostly from the state of Mato Grosso. Particularly beautiful are the **Bororo** and **Rikbaktsa** headdresses made from macaw and currasow feathers, and the **Kadiwéu** pottery (from Mato Grosso do Sul). Continuing along the road through the campus, signed on the left before a right turn in the road, is the **Zoológico** ① *Tue-Sun 0800-1100, 1330-1700, free*. The jacaré, capybara, tortoise and tapir pen can be seen at any time, but are best in the early morning or late afternoon. It also has coatis, otters, rhea, various monkeys and peccaries and a few, birds.

The **Águas Quentes** hot springs are 86 km away (9 km south of the BR-163, 77 km east of Cuiabá) and can be visited as a day trip.

The Northern Pantanal → *For listings, see pages 76-83. Colour map 3, A1 and A2.*

The Mato Grosso Pantanal is well-developed for tourism only along the Transpantaneira dirt road, which is superb for seeing wildlife – especially jaguars. Other areas around Barão do Melgaço and the colonial river port of Cáceres are pioneer country where you will probably not encounter another tourist.

The Transpantaneira

The main access point to the northern Pantanal is the **Transpantaneira dirt road**, which runs south from the main Cuiabá to Cáceres, beginning in earnest at the scruffy town of Poconé. The Transpantaneira cuts through the heart of the Pantanal wetland and is one of the best places for seeing wildlife in the Americas. Capybara, jaguarondi, oncilla, pacas and agoutis are common sights on the road itself, and the wetland areas immediately to either side – which begin as ditches and stretch into wilderness – are filled with hundreds of thousands of egrets, ibises, herons and metre-tall jabiru storks. Caiman bask on the banks of the ditches and ponds and anaconda snake their way through the water hyacinth and reeds. The road is lined with a string of *fazendas* (see page 76), of various levels of comfort, which are used by tour operators from Cuiabá as bases for deeper ventures into the wetlands.

The few towns that lie along the Transpantaneira are most interesting when seen from a wing mirror, but they do sell petrol. **Poconé** is an unprepossessing dusty little place, founded in 1781 and known as the 'Cidade Rosa' (pink city) by over-romantic locals. Until 1995 there was much *garimpo* (illicit gold mining) activity north of town and many slag heaps can be seen from the road. There are numerous cheap hotels in town but there is no real advantage in staying here. From Poconé it is 63 km (two to three hours) south to the one-horse town of **Pixaim**, where there is a petrol station, a few cafés and little else, and then a further two to three hours to **Porto Jofre**, at the end of the road and on the banks of the **Rio Piquiri**. The town is one of the best locations in the Americas for seeing jaguar and has a few hotels and restaurants. For information on visiting the Transpantaneira see Getting to the Brazilian Pantanal, page 6.

Barão de Melgaço and around → *Colour map 3, A2.*

Barão de Melgaço, 130 km from Cuiabá on the banks of the Rio Cuiabá, is far less visited than the Transpantaneira – you'll see far fewer tourists here, and far fewer animals. The

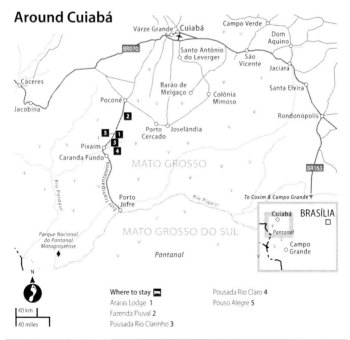

Around Cuiabá

Where to stay ◼
Araras Lodge 1
Fazenda Piuval 2
Pousada Rio Clarinho 3
Pousada Rio Claro 4
Pouso Alegre 5

Border essentials: Brazil–Bolivia

Cáceres (Brazil)–San Matías (Bolivia)

An unpaved road runs from Cáceres to the Bolivian border at San Matías. Exit and entry formalities are carried out at **Brazilian immigration**, Rua Col Farías, Cáceres, closed Sunday. When closed, go to the **Polícia Federal**, Avenida Rubens de Medarca 909. **Bolivian immigration** in San Matías is open 1000-1200, 1500-1700. If crossing from Bolivia into Brazil, there are three luggage checks for drugs before the border.

San Matías is a busy little town with hotels, restaurants and a bank. The next major town in Bolivia is San Ignacio de Velasco, which is on the road route to Santa Cruz de la Sierra. Buses run from San Matías to San Ignacio and San Ignacio to Santa Cruz; there are also flights. See Transport, page 83.

town sits on the edge of extensive areas of lakeland and seasonally flooded *cerrado*, and is reachable by two roads. The shorter, via Santo Antônio do Leverger, is unpaved from Santo Antônio to Barão (closed in the wet season). The route via São Vicente is longer but more extensively paved. The best way to see the Pantanal from here is by boat down the Rio Cuiabá. Near the town, the riverbanks are lined with farms and small residences but become increasingly forested with lovely combinations of flowering trees (best seen September to October); and the environs become increasingly wild and filled with birds, rodents and reptiles. After a while, a small river to the left leads to the **Chacororé** and **Sia Mariana lakes**, which join up via an artificial canal. The canal has resulted in the larger of the two lakes draining into the smaller one, and it has begun to dry out. Boats can continue beyond the lakes to the **Rio Mutum** but a guide is essential because there are many dead ends. The area is rich in birdlife and the waterscapes are beautiful.

Boat hire costs up to US$85 for a full day and is available from restaurants along the waterfront – ask at the **Restaurant Peixe Vivo**, or enquire with travel agencies in Cuiabá, who can organize a bespoke trip. The best time for a boat trip is sunset, when birds gather in huge numbers. Bring a powerful torch to do some caiman spotting for the return trip in the dark.

Cáceres → *For listings, see pages 76-83. Colour map 3, A1. Phone code: 065. Population: 86,000.*
Cáceres is a hot, steamy but hospitable provincial town on the far western edge of the Pantanal, sitting between the stunning **Serra da Mangabeira** mountains (15 km to the east), and the broad Rio Paraguai. The city is 200 km west of Cuiabá. It has little tourist infrastructure for Pantanal visits, but makes a possible pit stop on the long road between Cuiabá and Rondonia. It's a pleasant place, with a lovely waterfront and a number of well-preserved 19th-century buildings painted in pastel colours. It's easy to organize a short boat trip on the river. Until 1960, Cáceres used to have regular boat traffic downstream to the Rio de Plata. Occasional boats still run down river as far as Corumbá, and though there is no reliable service, if you're prepared to wait around for a few days you could probably hitch a ride. Travel in a pair or group if possible as the river route is a back door to Bolivia for cocaine traffickers.

The **Museu de Cáceres** ① *R Antônio Maria by Praça Major João Carlos*, is a small local history museum. Exhibits include indigenous funerary urns. The main square, **Praça Barão** de Rio Branco, has one of the original border markers from the Treaty of Tordesillas, which divided South America between Spain and Portugal. The *praça* is pleasant and shady during the day and, in the evenings between November and March, the trees are packed with thousands of chirping swallows (*andorinhas*); beware of droppings. The square is full of bars, restaurants and ice-cream parlours and comes to life at night. Vitória Regia lilies can be seen north of town, just across the bridge over the Rio Paraguai along the BR-174 and there are archaeological sites on the river's edge north of the city.

The Pantanal is wild near Cáceres, and was the site of a horrific jaguar attack in 2008 when a large female cat killed and partially ate a hunter. Excursions are difficult to organize, however, there is excellent wildlife and birdwatching in the Serra da Mangabeira – a steep, jagged range covered in forest and traversed by the BR-070 federal highway running from Cuiabá to Porto Velho.

Arriving in Cáceres The **rodoviária** ① *Terminal da Japonesa, T065-3224 1261*, has bus connections with Cuiabá and Porto Velho. It is also possible to arrive on the *Acuri*, a luxury boat that travels between Corumbá and Cuiabá. At the waterfront you can hire a boat for a day trip, US$5 per person per hour, minimum three people; on holidays and some weekends there are organized day trips on the river. ▸▸ *See Transport, page 83.*

The Chapada dos Guimarães and Nobres → For listings, see pages 76-83.
Colour map 3, A2. Phone code: 065. Population: 13,500. www.chapadadosguimaraes.com.br.

Although consumed by agriculture and blighted by ill-considered careless tourism development, the craggy, cave-pocked escarpments of the Chapada dos Guimarães constitute one of the oldest plateaux on earth and one of the most scenic areas in Mato Grosso. They are very easy to visit in a day trip from Cuiabá. They begin to rise from the hot plains around Cuiabá some 50 km from the city, forming a series of vertiginous stone walls washed by waterfalls and cut by canyons. A dramatic, winding road, the MT-020, ascends through one to an area of open savannah standing at around 700 m, broken by patches of *cerrado* forest and extensive areas of farmland, dotted with curiously eroded rocks, perforated by dripping caves and grottoes, and leading to whole series of viewpoints out over the dusty Mato Grosso plains. There is one small settlement, the tranquil and semi-colonial village of **Chapada dos Guimarães**, where life focuses on a single *praça* and people snooze through the week until the crowds rush in from Cuiabá on Fridays and Saturdays.

The Chapada is said to be the geodesic heart of the South American continent and, about 8 km east of Chapada dos Guimarães town, at the **Mirante do Ponto Geodésico**, there is a monument officially marking this. It overlooks a great canyon with views of the surrounding plains, the Pantanal and Cuiabá's skyline on the horizon.

As the geodesic centre, the highlands are rich with **New Age folklore**. Crystals tinkle in the shops in Chapada dos Guimarães village, and peyote people in tie-dye clothing gather in cafés to murmur about apocalypse and a new human evolution, over hot chocolate and soggy cake. The Chapada's rocks are said to have peculiar energizing properties; a fact more solidly grounded in truth than you may suspect – a local magnetic force that reduces the speed of cars has been documented here by the police.

The Chapada is pocked with caves. These include the **Caverna Arroe-jari** ⓘ *43 km of Chapada dos Guimarães village, daily 0900-1800, US$5, allow 3-4 hrs for the walk to and from the cave*, whose name means the 'home of souls' in a local Brazilian language. It's a haunting place – an 800-m-long cavern coursed by a little mountain stream running into a deep aqua blue lake, set in boulder-strewn grassland. It's best visited early in the day during the week, to ensure the fewest numbers of visitors possible, and to soak up the atmosphere. The walk to the cave cuts through waterfall-filled rainforest before emerging in open cerrado. Birdlife is rich.

The Chapada is a popular destination for birders, who often combine it with the Pantanal and Alta Floresta to up their species count. **Birdwatching** here is fruitful, in open country and with grassland and *cerrado* species not found in Alta Floresta and the Pantanal. Guides listed under the northern Pantanal (see page 81) can organize one- or two-day trips here and many are even based in the little town of Chapada dos Guimarães. Mammals, such as puma, jaguarundi, giant river otter and black-tailed marmoset can also be seen with time and patience.

Chapada dos Guimarães village

The colourful village of Chapada dos Guimarães, 68 km northeast of Cuiabá, is the most convenient and comfortable base for excursions. It's a pretty little place, with a series of simple, brightly painted buildings clustered around a small *praça* graced with the oldest church in the Mato Grosso, **Nossa Senhora de Santana**, dating from 1779 and with a simple whitewashed façade. It is open intermittently. Just outside the town, there's a big **piscina publica** ⓘ *R Dr Pem Gomes*, a spring-water fed, public swimming pool.

Arriving in Chapada dos Guimarães Frequent, regular buses run between Cuiabá and Chapada dos Guimarães village (about 1½ hours). The *chapada* can be visited in a long day trip either by self-drive (although access is via rough dirt roads that may deteriorate in the rainy season), bus or most easily through agencies such as **Pantanal Nature** or **Natureco** (see page 80). The **tourist office** ⓘ *R Quinco Caldas 100, 4 blocks from the praça*, near the entrance to the town, provides a useful map of the region and can help organize tours. The **Festival de Inverno** is held in the last week of July; during this time, and around **Carnaval**, the town is very busy and accommodation is scarce and expensive.

Parque Nacional da Chapada dos Guimarães

This begins just west of Chapada dos Guimarães town, near where the Salgadeira tourist centre offers bathing, camping and an unsightly restaurant right beneath the **Salgadeira waterfall**. The beautiful 85-m **Véu da Noiva waterfall** (Bridal Veil), 12 km from the town, near Buriti (well signposted; take a bus to Cuiabá and ask to be dropped you off), is less blighted and can be reached by either a short route or a longer one through forest. Other sights include: the **Mutuca** beauty spot, named after a vicious horsefly that preys on tourists there; the viewpoints over the breathtaking 80-m-deep **Portão do Inferno gorge** off the MT-020 road; and the **Cachoeirinha falls**, where there is another small, inappropriately situated restaurant.

About 60 km from town are the archaeological sites at **Pingador** and **Bom Jardim**, which include caverns with petroglyphs dating back some 4000 years.

Nobres and Bom Jardim

Some 100 km north of the Chapada is the little town of **Nobres**, which, like Bonito in Mato Grosso do Sul (see page 48), is surrounded by clear water rivers full of dourado fish and many beautiful caves. Unlike Bonito, there are few tourists and, whilst over-priced, the attractions are a good deal cheaper and far less spoilt. Nobres is the name for the area, but the main village, with a couple of small *pousadas* and a single restaurant, is called **Bom Jardim**. The town sits 2 km from the **Lago das Araras** ① *Bom Jardim, US$5*, a shallow lake surrounded by stands of buriti palm where hundreds of blue and yellow macaws roost overnight. Come at dawn for a wonderfully raucous dawn chorus. The restaurant **Estivado** ① *Rodovia MT-241, Km 66, 500 m northeast of Bom Jardim on the ponte Rio Estivado, US$4 for swimming (bring your own snorkel), US$7 for lunch*, offers a taste of what Nobres has to offer. It sits over the slow-flow of the Rio Esitvado, which forms a wide pool next to the restaurant and is filled with fish.

Nobres' other attractions dot the countryside around Bom Jardim, and as in Bonito they are on private ranch land. There is good snorkelling at the **Reino Encantado** ① *18 km from Bom Jardim at Alto Bela Vista, T065-9237 4471, US$50 for full day use including lunch, guide and equipment, US40 per night for a double room in the adjacent pousada*; the **Recanto Ecológico Lagoa Azul** ① *14 km from Bom Jardim at Alto Bela Vista, US$25 for entry, guide and equipment, US$8 extra for lunch*; and at the **Rio Triste** ① *18 km from Bom Jardim village, US$30 for a 2-hr float with guide and equipment rental*. The former two are half-kilometre floats down the Rio Salobra, which is filled with piraputanga (*Brycon microlepis*), piova (*Schizodon Borelli*) and piauçu (*Leporinus macrocephalus*) fish. The Rio Triste is filled with these species as well as fierce, salmon-like dourado (*Salminus maxillosus*) and spectacular mottled fresh-water stingrays, which should be treated with caution as they will inflict a painful wound if stepped on or handled. The most spectacular cave is the **Gruta do Lagoa Azul**, which was closed as this book went to press, and is set open according to the whims of **Ibama**, Brazil's environmental protection agency.

Visiting Nobres and Bom Jardim Bom Jardim town is served by a single daily bus from Cuiabá. However, there are at least four buses daily from Cuiabá (as well as services from Sinop and Alta Floresta) to Nobres town, from where there are regular connections to Bom Jardim. Taxis can be booked through the Pousada Bom Jardim to take visitors to the various attractions – there is no public transport. This can prove expensive (up to US$45 for a round trip to any single attraction, with waiting time), and the most practical way of visiting Nobres is with a tour agency in Cuiabá, such as **Pantanal Nature** or **Trip Nobres** (see page 80). The former can include the trip in conjunction with the Chapada dos Guimarães or Jardim da Amazônia and is better for wildlife.

The Mato Grosso Amazon → *For listings, see pages 76-83.*

Northern Mato Grosso is an enormous sea of soya which has washed much of the Amazon rainforest out of northern Mato Grosso under waves of agricultural expansion powered by the policies of the world's largest soya farmer, Mato Grosso's governor Blairo Maggi, who is number 62 on the Forbes power list. On ascending to the governorship of Mato Grosso, Maggi talked of tripling the area of soya planted in the Amazon. In an interview conducted with Larry Rohter of the *New York Times*, Maggi defended his destruction of the forest stating: "To me, a 40% increase in deforestation doesn't mean anything at all, and I don't feel the slightest guilt over what we are doing here. We're talking about an area larger than Europe that has barely been touched, so there is nothing at all to get worried about." He has been strongly supported by Lula, who declared in the same year that 'The Amazon is not untouchable', and is an ally of Lula's expansionist successor, Dilma Roussef. In 2003, Maggi's first year as governor, loggers cleared 4560 sq miles of Mato Grosso forest, an area twice the size of Delaware. The forests disappeared and Maggi profited: the André Maggi Group produces 5% of Brazil's soybeans and, with annual sales reaching US$2 billion in 2008, is the world's largest soy producer. Maggi received the Golden Chainsaw Award from Greenpeace international in 2005. Since exposure in the world's press, he has since attempted to re-invent himself as a champion of the environment, buying heavily into the carbon credit market. But the damage is largely done, and only islands of forest remain in northern Mato Grosso. Thankfully some are large.

The Xingu

The largest section of Mato Grosso forest by far is the indigenous reserves of the Xingu, which stretch into neighbouring Pará. These are home to dozens of tribal Brazilians, including the powerful Kayapó, and are protected under federal law since the indigenous cause was championed by the indefatigable Villas Boas brothers in the mid-20th century. The reserves are under threat from the Belo Monte dam – the third largest hydroelectric project in the world, which will alter the course of the Xingu river and prevent the migration of fish upriver, flood some 500 sq km of land and force some 40,000 indigenous and Caoboclo people to re-locate or become dependent on government handouts for food.

São Félix do Araguaia → *Colour map 1, C5. Population: 14,500.*

This town is the main population centre in the Mato Grosso Xingu region. It has a high population of indigenous Carajás, whose handicrafts can be found between the pizzeria and **Mini Hotel** on Avenida Araguaia. There is some infrastructure for fishing. Indigenous *fazenda* owners may invite you as their guest. If you accept, remember to take a gift: pencils, radio batteries, a few sacks of beans or rice, or a live cockerel will be much appreciated. Many river trips are available for fishing or wildlife spotting. ▸ *See What to do, page 82.*

Access to São Félix and Santa Teresinha is by bus from Cuiabá. The *rodoviária* is 3 km from the centre and waterfront, taxi US$15.

Jardim da Amazônia

Arriving at this private reserve by car is an incredible experience. The road from Cuiabá takes some five hours to drive, and is lined by soya, stretching to the horizon in every direction across the ceaseless plains. Thunderstorms flicker on the horizon and every hour or so you pass through a new agricultural town full of Stetsons and pick-ups. The turn-off to **Jardim da Amazônia** ① *300 km north of Cuiabá on the Rodovia MT-10, Km 88, São José do Rio Claro, Mato Grosso, T066-3386 1221, www.jdamazonia.com.br, book through Pantanal Nature to ensure you have a wildlife guide as they are not available at the reserve,* main road cuts immediately into thick forest. The horizon disappears and all is exuberant and full of life. Birds flit, paca and agouti run across the dirt road and, after a mile, forest clears to reveal a beautiful house, set in tropical gardens and sitting on a lake at the bend of a healthy Amazon river. Behind are a cluster of little boutiquey cabins. While it is entirely an island of forest (with no ecological corridors connecting it to the rest of the Amazon) the Jardim da Amazônia reserve is sufficiently large to maintain healthy populations of large neotropical mammals. There are jaguar and puma here, anaconda and giant otter. Capybara graze on the garden lawns at twilight and a tapir comes to steal cashew fruits from trees near the rooms in the dead of night. The reserve is also one of the few places in the Amazon to which you can safely bring children. It offers a range of activities, including canoeing on the river, rainforest walks and wildlife watching.

Cristalino Rainforest Reserve → *Phone code: 065. Colour map 1, B4. Population: 71,500.*
The road that runs due north from Cuiabá to Santarém (1777 km) is passable in all weather conditions as far as **Sinop**, and has recently been asphalted as far as **Santarém**. This will enable soya from Mato Grosso to be shipped via the Amazon to the Atlantic, out of a vast plant owned by **Cargill** but currently closed thanks to lobbying from Greenpeace Brazil. The areas around the road are among the principal victims of active deforestation, with land being cleared for cattle and soya farms. Soya is spreading beyond Mato Grosso into southern Pará.

There are, however, still extensive tracts of forest intact, especially near the **Rio Cristalino**, which is home to one of the Amazon's most spectacular rainforest reserves, the **Cristalino Rainforest Reserve** ⓘ *Alta Floresta, T066-3512 7100, www.cristalino lodge.com.br*. This is the best location in the Brazilian Amazon for wildlife enthusiasts, with superb guided visits to pristine rainforest, comfortable accommodation and wildlife-watching facilities as good as the best of Costa Rica or Ecuador. Cristalino is a private reserve the size of Manhattan. It is contiguous with the 184,940-ha **Cristalino State Park**, which is itself connected to other protected Amazon areas, forming an important large conservation corridor in the Southern Amazon. **Ecotourism** at Cristalino is a model of best practice and is streets ahead of anywhere else in Brazil. The management fulfill all four of the key conservational tourism criteria: conserving natural resources and biodiversity, conducting environmental education activities with the local community (leading to employment), practising responsible ecotourism (with recycling, water treatment, small group sizes and excellent guiding) and funding a research foundation.

Wildlife is abundant. Cristalino has so far recorded **600 bird species**, with new ones added almost monthly. This amounts to half of the avifauna in the Amazon and a third of all species found in Brazil. All the spectacular large mammals are found here alongside very rare or endemic species such as **bush dogs**, **red-nosed bearded saki monkey** and the recently-discovered **white-whiskered spider monkey**. And whilst wildlife is difficult to see (as it is anywhere in the Amazon), the reserve offers some of the best facilities for seeing wildlife in the Americas – on trail walks, boat trips on the river or from the lodge's enormous **birdiwatching tower**, which offers viewing in and above the forest canopy. There is also a hide next to a **clay lick** for seeing tapir, peccary and big cats, and harpy eagles nest in the grounds of the reserve's twin hotel, the **Floresta Amazônica** in Alta Floresta town. Scopes, binoculars and tape recorders are available and there is an excellent small library of field guides. The reserve also offers **adventure activities** including kayaking, rappelling and camping in the forest; sleeping in hammocks slung between the trees.

Visiting Cristalino Rainforest Reserve Cristalino is reachable from Alta Floresta town, which is connected to Cuiabá by regular buses and flights. The airport, **Aeroporto Deputado Benedito Santiago** ① *4 km from the city centre, Av Ariosto da Rivas s/n, T066-3521 2159*, has connections with both Cuiabá and Brasília with two of Brazil's larger airlines. There are also daily overnight buses from Cuiabá, 12 hours. The town was built in the late 1970s and laid out on a grid pattern. Finding your way around in straightforward. Cristalino Reserve representatives will meet you at the airport or bus station and transfer you to their hotels in the reserve by 4WD. Packages including transfers are available through the reserve's website.

Mato Grosso & the Northern Pantanal listings

For hotel and restaurant price codes and other relevant information, see pages 9-12.

For hotel and restaurant price codes and other relevant information, see pages 9-12.

▲here to stay

Cuiabá *p65, map p66*

$$$$ Amazon Plaza, Av Getúlio Vargas 600, T065-2121 2000, www.hotelamazon.com.br. By far the best in the centre with very smart modern rooms in a tower with good views. The chairs and decking in the relaxing, shady pool area are painted with pictures of Amazon wildlife. Excellent service. Broadband internet in all rooms.

$$$ Las Velas, Av Filinto Müller 62, Várzea Grande, T065-3682 3840, resvelas@terra.com.br. Less than 100 m from the airport. Clean, spacious a/c rooms (the executive ones are best and only a little more expensive) with newly renovated bathrooms, cable TV and boiler-heated showers. Free airport transfer for luggage.

$$ Mato Grosso, R Comandante Costa 643, T065-3614 7777, www.hotelmt.com.br. The best-value mid-range option in the centre with newly renovated a/c or fan-cooled rooms with tiled floors and chintzy beds, the brightest of which are on the 2nd floor or above.

$$ Nacional, Av Jules Rimet 22, T065-3621 3277. Opposite the front of the bus station and convenient for those who are just passing through. Plain a/c rooms with newly renovated en suites.

$$ Panorama, Praça Moreira Cabral 286, T065-3322 0072. A frayed 1980s tower with very simple, plain a/c or fan-cooled rooms with en suites; some have good views.

$$-$ HI Portal do Pantanal, Av Isaac Póvoas 655, T/F065-3624 8999, www.portaldopantanal.com.br. Large, bare dorms (segregated by sex) and doubles, a TV lounge area and a small kitchen. Price per person, breakfast included, internet access (US$2.50 per hr), laundry, kitchen.

$$-$ Hotel Ramos, R Campo Grande 487, T065 3624 7472, www.hotelramos.com.br. The best-value economy option with an array of well-kept, frayed but clean rooms, some with huge brown-tile bathrooms with tubs and showers, others with simple shower cubicles. These are set in a converted townhouse on a quiet, leafy back street close to the centre. Facilities include excellent tour agency, **Pantnanal Nature**, laundry service (with self-service machines), free Wi-Fi and airport/bus station pickup (with 12 hrs' notice). As with hostels, the lower price band for this hotel is per person.

$$-$ Ipanema, Av Jules Rimet 12, T065-3621 3069. Opposite the front of the bus station. Very well-kept a/c or fan-cooled rooms, some with armchairs, cable TVs and smart en suites. Internet access and a huge lobby TV for films or football. Many other options between here and the **Nacional**.

$$-$ Samara, R Joaquim Murtinho 270, T065-3322 6001. Very simple, scruffy rooms with en suite cold showers. No breakfast. Only come here if the other options are full.

The Northern Pantanal *p67*

Fazendas on the Transpantaneira

All prices here include tours around the *fazenda's* grounds with a guide – either on foot and or horseback or in a jeep, and full board.

See also page 57. Distances are given in kilometres from Poconé town. For tour operators, see What to do, page 80.

$$$$ Araras Lodge, Km 32, T065-3682 2800, www.araraslodge.com.br. Book direct or through **Pantanal Nature** or any of the other operators in Cuiabá as part of a tour. One of the most comfortable places to stay, with 14 a/c rooms. Excellent tours and food, home-made *cachaça*, a pool and a walkway over a private patch of wetland filled with capybara and caiman. Very popular with small tour groups from Europe. Book ahead.

$$$$ Fazenda Piuval, Km 10, T065-3345 1338, www.pousadapiuval.com.br. The 1st *fazenda* on the Transpantaneira and one of the most touristy, with scores of day visitors at weekends. Rustic farmhouse accommodation, a pool, excellent horseback and walking trails as well as boat trips on the vast lake, but whilst the *fazenda* is great for kids it's not a good choice for those looking to spot wildlife and really get into the sticks.

$$$$ Pousada Rio Clarinho, Km 42, book through **Pantanal Nature** (see page 81). Charming option on the Rio Clarinho. What it lacks in infrastructure, it makes up for in wildlife. The river has rare waterbirds such as agami heron and nesting hyacinth macaw, asTwell as river and giant otters and, occasionally, tapir. The boatman, Wander, has very sharp eyes – be sure to ask for him – and there is a 20-m birding tower in the grounds. Not to be confused with the nearby **Pousada Rio Claro** (see below).

$$$$ Pousada Rio Claro, Km 42, www.pousada rioclaro.com.br, book through **Eco do Pantanal** or **Natureco**. Comfortable *fazenda* with a pool and simple a/c rooms on the banks of the Rio Claro, which has a resident colony of giant otters. The *pousada* is most popular with Brazilian families and is very child-friendly; however, few Brazilians who visit here are as interested as in foreigners in seeing wildlife, or in the silent contemplation of pristine nature.

$$$$ Pouso Alegre, Km 36, T065-3626 1545, www.pousalegre.com.br. Rustic *pousada* with simple a/c or fan-cooled accommodation on one of the Pantanal's largest *fazendas*. It's overflowing with wildlife and particularly good for birds (especially on the morning horseback trail). Many new species have been catalogued here. The remote oxbow lake is particularly good for waterbirds (including agami and zigzag herons). The lodge is used by a number of

birding tour operators. Proper birding guides can be provided with advance notice. Best at weekends when the very knowledgeable owner Luís Vicente is there.

$$$-$$ Caranda Fundo, Km 43, book through **Pantanal Nature** (see page 81). One of the best options for budget travellers. Visitors sleep in hammocks in a large room (bring a hammock mosquito net). Tours include horseback rides, treks and night safaris. Hyacinth macaws nest on the *fazenda* and there are many mammals, including abundant howler monkeys, peccaries and huge herds of capybara.

Barão de Melgaço *p68*
There is a handful of cheaper options near the waterfront.

$$$$ do Mutum Pantanal Ecolodge, T065-3052 7022, www.pousada mutum.com.br, reservations through **Pantanal Nature**, or through other agencies in Cuiabá. One of the region's most comfortable lodges, with rooms housed in mock-colonial round houses or whitewash and tile-roofed cabins and set in a broad shady lawn around a lovely pool. The *pousada* organizes excursions on horseback around the surrounding Pantanal, or by jeep and by boat on the adjacent river.

$$ Pousada Baguari, R Rui Barbosa 719, Goiabeiras, Barão de Melgaço, T065-3322 3585. Rooms with a/c, restaurant, boat trips and excursions.

Cáceres *p69*
$$$ Caiçaras, R dos Operários 745 corner R Gen Osório, T065-3223 2234. Modern town hotel with a/c rooms and cheaper options without a fridge.

$$ Riviera Pantanal, R Gen Osório 540, T065-3223 1177, rivierapantanalhotel@ hotmail.com. Simple town hotel with a/c rooms, a pool and a restaurant.

$$-$ Charm, Col José Dulce 405, T/F065-3223 4949. A/c and fan-cooled rooms, with or without a shared bath.
$$-$ Rio, Praça Major João Carlos 61, T065-3223 3387. A range of rooms, the cheapest have shared bathrooms and no a/c.
$ União, R 7 de Setembro 340. Fan-cooled rooms, cheaper with shared bath, basic but good value.

The Chapada dos Guimarães *p70*
See www.chapadadosguimaraes.tur.br for further details.
$$$$ Pousada Penhasco, 2.5 km on Av Penhasco, Bom Clima, T065-3301 1555, www.penhasco.com.br. A medium-sized resort complex perched on the edge of the escarpment (for wonderful views), with modern chalets and bungalows, heated indoor and an outdoor pools (with waterslides), tennis courts and organized activities. A long way from quiet and intimate, but good for kids.
$$$ Solar do Inglês, R Cipriano Curvo 142, Centro, T065-3301 1389, www.solardoingles.com.br. In an old converted house near the town centre with 7 cosy rooms with dark wood floors, faux antiques and oriental rugs, each with private bathroom, TV and frigobar. Garden, swimming pool and sauna. Breakfast and afternoon tea included.
$$ Turismo, R Fernando Corrêa 1065, a block from the *rodoviária*, T065-3301 1176, www.hotelturismo.com.br. A/c rooms with a fridge, cheaper with fan, restaurant, breakfast and lunch excellent, very popular, German-run. Ralf Goebel, the owner, is very helpful in arranging excursions.
$$-$ Pousada Bom Jardim, Praça Bispo Dom Wunibaldo 461, T065-3301 2668. A bright, sunny reception in a colonial building on the main square leads to a corridor of either simple fan-cooled rooms or more comfortable a/c rooms painted light orange, and with wicker and wood furnishings, local art on the walls and private bathrooms.

$$-$ Rio's Hotel, R Tiradentes 333, T065-3301 1126, www.chapadadosguimaraes.com.br/pousadarios. Simple a/c doubles, triples and quadruples with a fridge, cheaper with fan, cheaper with shared bath and a good breakfast. Price in lower category is per person in a quadruple.
$$-$ São José, R Vereador José de Souza 50, T065-3301 1574, www.pousadasaojose.tur.br. This bright yellow cottage with a terracotta tiled roof just off the southeastern corner of the main square, and near the church, has an annexe of very plain fan-cooled or a/c singles, doubles with little more than a wardrobe and a bed (and a TV and fridge with a/c), and windows overlooking a small yard. The cheapest have shared bathrooms.

Camping
Oasis, 1 block from the main *praça*, T065-3301 2444, www.campingoasis.com.br. In an excellent central location in the large lawned garden dotted with fruit trees and sitting behind a townhouse. Facilities include separate bathrooms for men and women, cooking facilities and a car park.

Nobres *p72*
$$-$ Pousada Bom Jardim and Bom Garden, Vila Bom Jardim, T065-3102 2018, www.pousadabomjardim.com. 2 hotels joined as 1 – **Bom Garden** – out the back has modern, well-kept a/c rooms with en suites and TVs, **Bom Jardim** is simpler, with less-well-appointed, older and smaller rooms. The restaurant has a central restaurant and can organize tours (though no English is spoken).

São Félix do Araguaia *p73*
$$ Xavante, Av Severiano Neves 391, T062-3522 1305. A/c, frigobar, excellent breakfast, delicious *cajá* juice, the owners are very hospitable. Recommended.
$ Pizzeria Cantinho da Peixada, Av Araguaia, next to the Texaco station,

overlooking the river, T062-3522 1320. Rooms to let by the owner of the restaurant, better than hotels. He also arranges fishing trips.

Cristalino Rainforest Reserve *p74*

$$$$ Cristalino Jungle Lodge, reservations Av Perimetral Oeste 2001, Alta Floresta, T065-3512 7100, www.cristalinolodge.com.br. A beautifully situated and well-run lodge on the Cristalino river in a private reserve the size of Manhattan island. This reserve is contiguous with the 185,000-ha Cristalino State Park (which is linked to other protected areas to form a huge conservation corridor in the Southern Amazon). Trips from the lodge include canoeing and snorkelling in clear-water rivers, as well as the usual caiman spotting and piranha fishing as well as more adventurous options such as rapelling and canyoning. But the emphasis is on wildlife, with more than 600 species of birds (half of the avifauna in the Amazon and a third of all species found in Brazil) and unique mammals such as the newly discovered white-whiskered spider monkey as well as very rare species like jaguar, puma, tapir, bush dog and giant otter. Facilities are the best in the Amazon – with a library of wildlife books, scopes and binoculars, canoes and launches, a 50-m canopy lookout tower and superb guiding. The lodge supports the local community, practices recycling and water treatment and funds a scientific research programme.

$$ Floresta Amazônica, Av Perimetral Oeste 2001, Alta Floresta, T065-3521 3601. In the park with lovely views, pool, sports, all facilities.

$$ Pirâmide Palace, Av do Aeroporto 445, Alta Floresta, T065-3521 2400. A/c rooms with fridges, restaurant.

$ Grande Hotel Coroados, R F1 No118, Alta Floresta, T065-3521 3022. Not very well kept but has a/c, pool and bar.

Restaurants

Cuiabá *p65, map p66*

Many of the restaurants in the centre are only open weekdays for lunch. On **Av CPA** there are many good restaurants and small snack bars. **R Jules Rimet**, across from the *rodoviária*, has several cheap restaurants and *lanchonetes*.

$$$ Getúlio, Av Getúlio Vargas 1147, at São Sebastião, T065-3264 9992. An a/c haven to escape from the heat. Black-tie waiters, excellent food with meat specialities and pizza, and a good buffet lunch on Sun. Live music upstairs on Fri and Sat from significant Brazilian acts.

$$$-†† Choppão, Praça 8 de Abril, T065-3623 9101. Established 30 years ago, this local institution is buzzing at any time of day or night. Huge portions of delicious food or *chopp*. The house speciality chicken soup promises to give diners drinking strength in the early hours and is a meal in itself. Warmly recommended.

$$ Panela de Barro, R Cmte Costa 543. Self-service, a/c lunchtime restaurant with a choice of tasty regional dishes.

$$-† Miranda's, R Cmte Costa 716. Decent self-service per kg lunchtime restaurant with good value specials.

Cáceres *p69*

$$ Corimbá, R 15 de Novembro s/n, on the riverfront. Fish and general Brazilian food.

$ Gulla's, R Col José Dulce 250. Per kg buffet, good quality and variety. Recommended.

$ Panela de Barro, R Frei Ambrósio 34, near the *rodoviária*. Brazilian *comida caseira* (home cooking) with the usual range of meat dishes with squash, rice, black beans and salads.

Chapada dos Guimarães p70

Pequi is a regional palm fruit with a deadly spiky interior used to season many foods; *arroz com pequi* is a popular local rice and chicken dish.

$$ Fellipe 1, R Cipriano Curvo 596, T065-3301 1793. One of the few per kilo restaurants in the village, on the south-western corner of the square next to the church serving mostly meaty options, beans, rice, unseasoned salads and sticky puddings. In the evenings, the menu becomes à la carte.

$$ Nivios, Praça Dom Wunibaldo 631. A popular spot for meat and regional food.

Nobres p72

$ WF, T065-3102 2020. Lunch every day and dinner with reservation only from Senhora Fatima who serves a hearty meal of meat/chicken/fish with beans, rice, salad and condiments, washed down with fresh tropical fruit juice.

São Félix do Araguaia p73

$$ Pizzeria Cantinho da Peixada, Av Araguaia, next to the Texaco station, overlooking the river. As well as serving pizza, the owner, Klaus, also rents rooms.

Bars and clubs

Cuiabá p65, map p66

Cuiabá is quite lively at night, bars with live music and dance on Av CPA.

Café Cancun, R Candido Mariano at São Sebastião. One of a chain of popular Brazilian club-bars attracting a mid-20s to 40s crowd.

Choppão, see Restaurants, above.

Tucano, Av CPA. Daily 1800-2300. Restaurant-bar specializing in pizza, with beautiful view.

Entertainment

Cáceres p69

Traditional folkloric dance groups: **Chalana**, T065-3223 3317, and **Tradição**, T065-223 4505, perform shows at different locations.

Festivals

Cáceres p69

Mid-Mar Piranha Festival.

Mid-Sep International Fishing Festival. There's also an annual cattle fair.

Shopping

Cuiabá p65, map p66

Local handicrafts in wood, straw, netting, leather, skins, Pequi liquor, crystallized caju fruit, compressed guaraná fruit and indigenous crafts are on sale at the airport, *rodoviária*, craft shops in the centre and at the daily market in the Praça da República, interesting. There's a picturesque fish and vegetable market at the riverside.

Casa de Artesão, Praça do Expedicionário 315, T065-3321 0603. All types of local crafts in a restored building.

The Chapada dos Guimarães p70

Ispiaaió, R Cipriano Curvo, Praça Dom Wunibaldo, T065-9214 8420. Regional arts and crafts, including mobiles (of the hanging from the ceiling variety), wall hangings, lacework and clothing.

What to do

Cuiabá p65, map p66

Travel agencies in Cuiabá also offer trips to the *chapada*.

Tours to the northern Pantanal

You should expect to pay US$70-100 per person per day for tours in the Pantanal. Budget trips are marginally more expensive (around US$10-15 per day more) than those in the southern Pantanal, but accommodation in the *fazendas* is more comfortable. For longer tours or special programmes, book in advance and be very wary of cut-price cowboy operators, some of whom hang around in the airport alongside those we list below.

Ecoverde Tours, R Pedro Celestino 391, Centro, T065-9638 1614 or 3624 1386, www.ecoverdetours.com.br. No-frills, but well-run backpacker tours of the Pantanal with Joel Souza, who has many years guiding experience, knows his birds and beasts and speaks good English. Ask if he is available as other guides are not always of the same standard. The best option in Cuiabá for a budget trip to the Pantanal.

Natureco, R Benedito Leite 570, Cuiabá, T065-3321 1001, www.natureco.com.br. A range of *fazenda*-based Pantanal tours, trips to the Xingu, Cáceres, Alta Floresta and Barão de Melgaco. Specialist wildlife guides available with advance notice. Some English spoken. Professional and well run.

Pantanal Nature Tours, R Campo Grande 487, Centro, T065-3322 0203, T065-9955 2632 (mob), www.pantanalnature.com.br. Great trips to the northern Pantanal – both to the *fazendas* along the Transpantaneira and to Porto Jofre, from where the company runs the best jaguar safari in the Pantanal, and to Nobres, the Chapada dos Guimarães and Pousada Jardim da Amazônia. Guiding is excellent (bilingual) and service professional.

Pantanal wildlife and birding guides

All guides work freelance; companies employ extra guides for trips when busy. Most guides wait at the airport for incoming flights; compare prices and services in town if you don't want to commit yourself. The tourist office recommends guides, however, their advice is not always impartial. Those recommended below can be booked with advance notice through **Eco do Pantanal** or **Natureco**.

Ailton Lara, T065-3322 0203, ailton@pantanal nature.com.br. Excellent and good-value birding trips to the Chapada, the Pantanal and other destinations around Mato Grosso.

Boute Expeditions, R Getúlio Vargas 64, Várzea Grande, near airport, T065-3686 2231, www.boute-expeditions.com. Paulo Boute is one of the most experienced birding guides in the Pantanal; works from home and speaks good English and French. His standard tours operate in Mato Grosso (including the Amazon and the Chapada alongside the Pantanal). He also runs tours to the Atlantic coastal forests and other bespoke destinations on request.

Fabricio Dorileo, fabriciodorileo18@ yahoo.com.br or through Eduardo Falcão – rejaguar@bol.com.br. Excellent birding guide with good equipment, good English and many years' experience in the Pantanal and Chapada dos Guimarães. Trained in the USA. Book him through the Cuiabá operators.

Giuliano Bernardon, T065-8115 6189, T065-9982 1294, giubernardon@gmail.com. Young birding guide and photographer with a good depth of knowledge and experience in the Chapada, Pantanal, Mato Grosso, Amazon and Atlantic coastal forest.

Pantanal Bird Club, T065-3624 1930, www.pantanalbirdclub.org. Recommended for even the most exacting clients, PBC are the most illustrious birders in Brazil with many years of experience. Braulio Carlos, the owner, has worked with Robert Ridgely and Guy Tudor and his chief guide, Juan Mazar Barnett, is one of the editors of *Cotinga* magazine. Tours throughout the area and to various parts of Brazil.

The Chapada dos Guimarães *p70*

Chapada Pantanal, Av Fernando Correa da Costa 1022, T065-3301 2757. Tours to all the principal sights in the Chapada and trips further afield to Nobres.

Nobres *p72*

The Cuiabá agencies listed under the Pantanal, and **Chapada Pantanal Tours** in Chaoda dos Guimaraes village visit Nobres. **Pantanal Nature** (see above). Trips to all the attractions in Nobres. These can be combined with the Chapada dos Guimarães and Jardim da Amazonia. Excellent for wildlife.

Trip Nobres, T065-3023 6080, www.tripnobres.com. Boisterous light adventure activities in and around Nobres, including abseiling, rafting, snorkelling and diving. The owner is one of the few PADI-accredited dive instructors in the area.

São Félix do Araguaia *p73*

Boat trips

Icuryala, Goiânia, T062-223 9518. Excellent food and service, US$100 per day, independent visitors welcome. Recommended. **Juracy Lopes**, contact through **Hotel Xavante** (see page 78). A very experienced guide with many friends, including the chief and council in Santa Isabela. Trips to the village or to see wildlife cost US$15 for 2; longer trips can be made to the meeting of the waters with the Rio das Mortes, or for a night in the jungle.

⊖ Transport

Cuiabá *p65, map p66*

Air Marechal Rondon international airport is 10 km from the city; taxi US$18, or take the white Tuiuiú bus from Av Tenente Coronel Duarte in the city centre, US$1.50, or the terminal. There are also aeroporto buses from the rodoviária. Flights can be booked in the airline offices at the airport or through **Pantanal Nature**, or other tour operators in town, which also handle bus tickets. Cuibá has connections with **Alta Floresta, Belo Horizonte, Brasília, Campo Grande,** **Curitiba, Foz de Iguaçu, Goiânia, Manaus, Salvador, Santarem, Porto Alegre, Porto Velho, Salvador, São Paulo, Rio de Janeiro** and onward connections, with **Asta**, www.voeasta.com.br, **Avianca**, www.Avianca.com.br, **Azul**, www.voeazul.com.br, **GOL**, www.voegol.com.br, **Pantanal**, www.voepantanal.com.br, **Passaredo**, www.voepassaredo.com.br, **TAM**, www.tam.com.br and **TRIP**, www.voetrip.com.br.

Bus Bus No 202 runs to the *rodoviária* from R Joaquim Murtinho by the cathedral, 20 mins. A taxi costs US$10 to the centre. There is a Bradesco ATM, cafés and restaurants in the *rodoviária*.

Buses to **Alta Floresta**, 3 daily, 12 hrs, US$85; **Brasília**, 2 daily morning and evening, 18 hrs, US$90; **Campo Grande**, 12 hrs, 12 daily, US$55-65; **Foz de Iguaçu**, 2, both in the small hours, 23 hrs, US$100-115; **Goiânia**, 5 daily, 15 hrs, US$75; **Palmas**, 1 daily, 25 hrs, US$110 (via Goiânia); **Porto Velho**, 3 daily, US$75, 23 hrs; **Rio**, 36 hrs, US$150; **Salvador**, on Mon, Wed and Fri, 48 hrs, US$150; **Santarem**, 1 daily, 48 hrs, US$140; **Rio Branco**, 1 daily, 37 hrs, US$100 (or change in Porto Velho); **São Paulo**, 2 daily US$85-95, 24 hrs.

Car hire Atlântida, Av Isaac Póvoas, T065-3623 0700. **Localiza**, Av Dom Bosco 965, T065-3624 7979, and at airport, T065-3682 7900. **Unidas**, airport, T065-3682 4062. Vitória, R Comandante Costa 1350, T065-3322 7122.

The Transpantaneira *p67*

Bus From Poconé to **Cuiabá**, US$10 with **TUT**, T065-3322 4985, 6 a day 0600-1900.

Car Poconé has a 24-hr petrol station with all types of fuel, but closed on Sun.

Border with Bolivia *p69*
Bus From Cáceres to **San Matías**,
US$20 with **Transical-Velásquez**, Mon-Sat
at 0630 and 1500, Sun 1500 only (return
at same times). **Trans Bolivia** to **San Matías**,
Sun, Mon, Fri at 1500, Tue, Wed, Thu and Sat
at 0700. For details of crossing the border,
see box, page 69.

Cáceres *p69*
Bus **Colibrí/União Cascavel** buses
to **Cuiabá**, US$15, many daily 0630-2400
from the *rodoviária* (book in advance, very
crowded), 3½ hrs. To **Porto Velho**, US$50.

Boat Intermittent sailings to Corumbá –
ask at the docks when you arrive.

Car hire **Localiza**, R Padre Cassimiro 630,
T065-3223 1330, and at airport. **Locavel**,
Av São Luís 300, T065-3223 1212.

Chapada dos Guimarães *p70*
Bus 7 departures daily to **Cuiabá** (Rubi,
0700-1900, last return 1800), 1½ hrs, US$5.

Nobres *p72*
See Visiting Nobres and Bom Jardim, page 72.

São Félix do Araguaia *p73*
Bus To **Barra do Garças** at 0500, arrive
2300; or 1730, arrive 1100 next day. Also
to **Tucumã**, 6-8 hrs, and to **São José do
Xingu**, 10 hrs. No buses to Marabá.

Jardim da Amazônia *p73*
With tour operators from Cuiabá only –
or self drive. **Pantanal Nature**, page 81,
are the best option.

Cristalino Rainforest Reserve *p74*

Alta Floresta
Air Cristalino Jungle Lodge offers a free
pick-up and drop-off for guests. There's little
reason to come if you're not going to the
lodge. There are flights to **Brasília**, **Cuiabá**,
Curitiba, **Porto Alegre**, **Campinas**,
Cascaval, **Ji-Paraná**, **Londrina**, **Maringá**,
Rondonópolis, **Sinop** and **Vilhena**,
with **Avianca**, www.Avianca.com.br,
or **Trip**, www.voetrip.com.br.

Bus To **Cuiabá** daily, several (12 hrs, US$35).
The *leito* night bus is the best option.

ℹ Directory

Cuiabá *p65, map p66*
Banks **Banco do Brasil**, Av Getúlio Vargas
and R Barão de Melgaço, commission US$10
for cash, US$20 per transaction for TCs (there
are several branches of **Bradesco**, R Barão
Melgaco 3435, for ATMs.

Cáceres *p69*
Banks **Banco do Brasil**, R Col Jose Dulcé 234.
HSBC, R Col Jose Dulcé 145. **Casa de Câmbio
Mattos**, Comte Bauduino 180,
next to main *praça*, changes cash and
TCs at good rates.

The Chapada dos Guimarães *p70*
Banks **Bradesco** R Fernando Correia 868
With an ATM. **Post office** R Fernando
Corrêa 848.

Contents

Footnotes

Index

Titles available in the Footprint *Focus* range

Latin America	UK RRP	US RRP
Bahia & Salvador	£7.99	$11.95
Brazilian Amazon	£7.99	$11.95
Brazilian Pantanal	£6.99	$9.95
Buenos Aires & Pampas	£7.99	$11.95
Cartagena & Caribbean Coast	£7.99	$11.95
Costa Rica	£8.99	$12.95
Cuzco, La Paz & Lake Titicaca	£8.99	$12.95
El Salvador	£5.99	$8.95
Guadalajara & Pacific Coast	£6.99	$9.95
Guatemala	£8.99	$12.95
Guyana, Guyane & Suriname	£5.99	$8.95
Havana	£6.99	$9.95
Honduras	£7.99	$11.95
Nicaragua	£7.99	$11.95
Northeast Argentina & Uruguay	£8.99	$12.95
Paraguay	£5.99	$8.95
Quito & Galápagos Islands	£7.99	$11.95
Recife & Northeast Brazil	£7.99	$11.95
Rio de Janeiro	£8.99	$12.95
São Paulo	£5.99	$8.95
Uruguay	£6.99	$9.95
Venezuela	£8.99	$12.95
Yucatán Peninsula	£6.99	$9.95

Asia	UK RRP	US RRP
Angkor Wat	£5.99	$8.95
Bali & Lombok	£8.99	$12.95
Chennai & Tamil Nadu	£8.99	$12.95
Chiang Mai & Northern Thailand	£7.99	$11.95
Goa	£6.99	$9.95
Gulf of Thailand	£8.99	$12.95
Hanoi & Northern Vietnam	£8.99	$12.95
Ho Chi Minh City & Mekong Delta	£7.99	$11.95
Java	£7.99	$11.95
Kerala	£7.99	$11.95
Kolkata & West Bengal	£5.99	$8.95
Mumbai & Gujarat	£8.99	$12.95

Africa & Middle East	UK RRP	US RRP
Beirut	£6.99	$9.95
Cairo & Nile Delta	£8.99	$12.95
Damascus	£5.99	$8.95
Durban & KwaZulu Natal	£8.99	$12.95
Fès & Northern Morocco	£8.99	$12.95
Jerusalem	£8.99	$12.95
Johannesburg & Kruger National Park	£7.99	$11.95
Kenya's Beaches	£8.99	$12.95
Kilimanjaro & Northern Tanzania	£8.99	$12.95
Luxor to Aswan	£8.99	$12.95
Nairobi & Rift Valley	£7.99	$11.95
Red Sea & Sinai	£7.99	$11.95
Zanzibar & Pemba	£7.99	$11.95

Europe	UK RRP	US RRP
Bilbao & Basque Region	£6.99	$9.95
Brittany West Coast	£7.99	$11.95
Càdiz & Costa de la Luz	£6.99	$9.95
Granada & Sierra Nevada	£6.99	$9.95
Languedoc: Carcassonne to Montpellier	£7.99	$11.95
Málaga	£5.99	$8.95
Marseille & Western Provence	£7.99	$11.95
Orkney & Shetland Islands	£5.99	$8.95
Santander & Picos de Europa	£7.99	$11.95
Sardinia: Alghero & the North	£7.99	$11.95
Sardinia: Cagliari & the South	£7.99	$11.95
Seville	£5.99	$8.95
Sicily: Palermo & the Northwest	£7.99	$11.95
Sicily: Catania & the Southeast	£7.99	$11.95
Siena & Southern Tuscany	£7.99	$11.95
Sorrento, Capri & Amalfi Coast	£6.99	$9.95
Skye & Outer Hebrides	£6.99	$9.95
Verona & Lake Garda	£7.99	$11.95

North America	UK RRP	US RRP
Vancouver & Rockies	£8.99	$12.95

Australasia	UK RRP	US RRP
Brisbane & Queensland	£8.99	$12.95
Perth	£7.99	$11.95

For the latest books, e-books and a wealth of travel information, visit us at: www.footprinttravelguides.com.

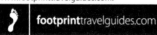

Join us on facebook for the latest travel news, product releases, offers and amazing competitions: www.facebook.com/footprintbooks.